Fertile ground

Fertile ground

Che Guevara and Bolivia

A firsthand account by Rodolfo Saldaña

PATHFINDER

NEW YORK LONDON MONTREAL SYDNEY

3 1257 01393 8930

Edited by Mary-Alice Waters

Copyright © 1997, 2001 by Pathfinder Press

ISBN 0-87348-923-3 paper; ISBN 0-87348-924-1 cloth
Library of Congress Catalog Card Number 00-136387

Manufactured in the United States of America

First edition, 2001

COVER DESIGN: Eva Braiman
FRONT COVER PHOTO: AP/Wide World Photos
BACK COVER PHOTO: Courtesy Gladys Brizuela

Pathfinder
> 410 West Street, New York, NY 10014, U.S.A.
> Fax: (212) 727-0150
> E-mail: pathfinderpress@compuserve.com

PATHFINDER DISTRIBUTORS AROUND THE WORLD:

Australia (and Asia and the Pacific):
> Pathfinder, 1st floor, 176 Redfern St., Redfern, NSW 2016
> Postal address: P.O. Box K879, Haymarket, NSW 1240

Canada:
> Pathfinder, 2761 Dundas St. West, Toronto, ON, M6P 1Y4

Iceland:
> Pathfinder, Klapparstíg 26, 2d floor, 101 Reykjavík
> Postal address: P. Box 0233, IS 121 Reykjavík

New Zealand:
> Pathfinder, La Gonda Arcade, 203 Karangahape Road, Auckland
> Postal address: P.O. Box 8730, Auckland

Sweden:
> Pathfinder, Vikingagatan 10, S-113 42, Stockholm

United Kingdom (and Europe, Africa except South Africa, and Middle East):
> Pathfinder, 47 The Cut, London, SE1 8LL

United States (and Caribbean, Latin America, and South Africa):
> Pathfinder, 410 West Street, New York, NY 10014

Contents

Rodolfo Saldaña

RODOLFO SALDAÑA was a founding member of the ELN (National Liberation Army) of Bolivia, led by Ernesto Che Guevara and Bolivian revolutionary Inti Peredo. Saldaña was among the initial Bolivian cadres of the 1966–67 revolutionary front in that country and was slated to join the guerrilla effort as a combatant. His responsibilities in face of the vicissitudes of the guerrilla front, however, kept him at the head of the ELN's underground network in the cities and tin mining regions. In this capacity, he organized to recruit fighters among working people and youth, particularly miners, as well as provide logistical support to the guerrillas. Following the death of Guevara and most of the remaining combatants in October 1967, Saldaña worked to consolidate new forces in Bolivia and relaunch the revolutionary struggle.

Born March 29, 1932, in Sucre, Bolivia, Saldaña spent his childhood in the Cinti region, where his mother worked a small plot of land together with her brother. Saldaña grew up speaking both Spanish and Quechua, the language of the large majority of Bolivia's indigenous population.

He became active in politics as a high school student. In 1950 he joined the newly formed Communist Party of Bolivia and was a founder and leader of the Bolivian Communist Youth. As a student leader in the early 1950s, he attended international meetings of the World Federation of Democratic Youth. In 1953 he graduated from the polytechnic institute of La Paz and the following year enrolled in engineering at the University of San

Andrés there, soon dropping out to engage in political work.

From 1955 to 1958, by decision of the party, Saldaña worked in the Siglo XX tin mine, Bolivia's largest, where he was instrumental in recruiting leaders of the mineworkers and establishing the Communist Party in the mines. He became a leader of the Federation of Mine Workers of Bolivia (FSTMB) and participated in numerous national meetings of the miners union as well as the Bolivian Workers Federation (COB). He was elected to the Central Committee of the party.

Following the victory of the Cuban Revolution in 1959, Rodolfo Saldaña became actively involved in supporting the broadening and accelerating revolutionary struggles throughout Latin America. He took part in logistical preparations and support work for both the 1963 Peruvian guerrilla movement defeated at Puerto Maldonado, and the 1963–64 Argentine guerrilla front led by Jorge Ricardo Masetti.

In late 1965 Saldaña and several other CP cadres went to Cuba, where they requested and, with the agreement of the Bolivian Communist Party leadership, received military training. On returning to Bolivia in July 1966, they began preparations for what would later that year become the guerrilla front commanded by the Argentine-Cuban leader Ernesto Che Guevara. A few weeks after Guevara's arrival in November 1966, Saldaña met with him at the guerrillas' base camp on the Ñancahuazú river. Saldaña left the Communist Party in the fall of 1966, when the party leadership, under the direction of its general secretary Mario Monje, refused to support the effort led by Guevara.

Following the eleven-month guerrilla campaign, Saldaña received further military training in Cuba in 1969 and returned clandestinely to Bolivia. Arrested by the dictatorship in May 1970, he was freed in July in exchange for employees of a U.S. gold-mining company who had been taken hostage by the ELN. He subsequently received asylum in Cuba.

From 1970 to 1983 Saldaña lived in Cuba, collaborating with the Organization of Solidarity with the Peoples of Asia, Africa and Latin America (OSPAAAL), the Latin American Continental Organization of Students (OCLAE), and the Cuban Institute for Friendship with the Peoples (ICAP). He worked for Radio Havana, where he broadcast to Bolivia in Quechua and translated other materials into that language. He also graduated with a degree in sociology from the University of Havana.

In 1983, following the end of the series of military dictatorships in Bolivia, Saldaña returned. He was a founder of the Bolivian-Cuban Cultural and Friendship Association and taught at the University of San Andrés in La Paz. In 1990 he moved back to Cuba, where he worked at the news agency InterPress Service and at Radio Havana.

Rodolfo Saldaña died in Havana on June 29, 2000.

Harry Villegas, the author of the foreword, was a member of the general staff of the 1966-67 revolutionary front in Bolivia led by Ernesto Che Guevara. Known also by his nom de guerre *Pombo,* Villegas led the surviving veterans of the guerrilla campaign out of a massive encirclement organized by the Bolivian army and their U.S. advisers. With the help of Bolivian revolutionaries, Villegas and four others were able to escape; the three Cuban survivors eventually crossed the border to Chile and returned to Cuba. The individuals and events Villegas refers to are touched on by Saldaña in the interview that follows.

Between 1975 and 1990 Villegas was at the center of the successful efforts by the internationalist volunteers of Cuba's Revolutionary Armed Forces to help the government of Angola defeat the invading forces of the apartheid regime in South Africa and imperialism's campaign to overthrow the newly independent Angolan regime. As a teenager, Villegas joined the Rebel Army commanded by Fidel Castro. Today he holds the rank of brigadier general in the Revolutionary Armed Forces and is a Hero of the Republic of Cuba. He is a member of the Central Committee of the Communist Party of Cuba, a delegate to the National Assembly, and serves as a national leader of the Association of Combatants of the Cuban Revolution.

Foreword

IN WRITING THESE LINES I am fulfilling two duties. First, invoking the memory of a friend and comrade with whom I shared many revolutionary actions. Second, responding to the request by Hero of the Republic of Cuba, Army Corps General Abelardo Colomé Ibarra, who was a comrade of Rodolfo Saldaña in the latter's revolutionary work going back to the 1960s.

"With them came Rodolfo, who made a very good impression on me. He seems more determined than Bigote to break with everything. Papi informed him of my presence." This is what Commander Ernesto Che Guevara wrote in his field diary in Bolivia on November 20, 1966. The following day he noted, "I asked Rodolfo to send us an agronomist who can be trusted."

The interview with this outstanding Bolivian combatant conducted by Mary-Alice Waters and Mike Taber offers a close-up, human view of a long record of intense revolutionary battles beginning in 1950.

Loyalty, firmness, modesty, solidarity, humility, and dedication to the freedom of the peoples. These are words that define the life of the communist Rodolfo Saldaña.

Cuban revolutionaries are aware that starting in 1963 Saldaña gave full support to Che's plans to open a guerrilla front in Salta, Argentina, as well as to the movement in Puerto Maldonado, Peru. This is yet further evidence of his Latin American patriotism, of his opposition to imperialism, always in search of attaining true freedom.

Whether as student, mine worker, auto mechanic, teacher, member of the Bolivian Communist Party and its Central Committee, or leader of the urban network of the National Liberation Army of Bolivia, what characterized Saldaña was his honesty, personal example, and faithfulness to principles. In reality he reached what Che called "the highest level attained by the human species," that of being a revolutionary.

His incorporation into the Bolivian guerrilla front—for which he had received training beginning in January 1966—was prevented by factors beyond his control and choice. These included the necessity both of Tania's trip to the guerrilla front and then of her remaining there, which meant he had to continue his work in the city. Another factor, resulting from the Bolivian army's cordon around the zone of operations, was that contact with the guerrilla front and with Cuba was lost, despite efforts by the urban network to reestablish lines of communication. Unfortunately, Che never knew of these efforts.

In face of the treacherous stance by Mario Monje, general secretary of the Bolivian Communist Party, Saldaña was compelled to leave the party he helped found, and that, from the time he was very young, had changed the course of his life. Saldaña's firm decision to follow Che must have been very difficult and painful. But with integrity and conviction, he was prepared to implement this decision, adopted completely and without hesitation, because he was conscious of the full liberating dimension of Che's actions.

A few words on a personal note. We experienced Saldaña's solidarity and comradeship after we had evaded the encirclement of ten thousand Bolivian troops. We were in Cochabamba at the time, and knowledge of our presence in that city was spreading through "Radio Bemba," as we say in Cuba, that is, by word of mouth.

The compañeros of the National Liberation Army in La Paz, on their own and without the support of the Bolivian Communist Party leadership, decided to come find us. With joy and surprise one night, I saw three compañeros arrive, Rodolfo among them. "Compañero, we've come to rescue all of you," he told me, and we were taken to La Paz. Arriving at the house where we were to be hidden, we noticed two soldiers coming toward our car. Seeing us reach for our revolvers, Rodolfo touched my hand and said, "Easy, it's beyond their imagination that you could be here," giving us a demonstration of courage, dependability, and composure.

Later in Cuba, under the leadership of Guido (*Inti*) Peredo, the survivors of the October 8, 1967, battle at the Yuro Ravine underwent military training. The objective was to fulfill our commitment to continue the struggle. With great resolve and dedication, Saldaña trained alongside Bolivian, Chilean, and Cuban revolutionaries. His uppermost objective was always to "return to the mountains" in order to obtain the victory of the people of Bolivia and of the Americas.

While living in Cuba he participated in the revolution and felt fulfillment in being a builder of socialism. This was the great dream of a life dedicated entirely to the working people, with the working people, and for the working people.

Following Rodolfo Saldaña's recent death in Havana, his remains were returned to his Bolivian homeland. The publication of this valuable testimony, left by him as a legacy, constitutes a posthumous tribute to a vanguard combatant, a man faithful to the ideas to which he dedicated his life.

Hasta la victoria siempre.

Harry Villegas Tamayo
Havana, January 18, 2001

Introduction

This great mass of humanity has said, "Enough!"
and has begun to march.

February 4, 1962
Second Declaration of Havana

THE TRIUMPH of the Cuban Revolution was not an isolated event. It was part of a rising wave of anti-imperialist struggles throughout the Americas, struggles that in turn drew new strength from the example set by the workers and farmers of Cuba. The upheavals that marked the class struggle in Bolivia from the 1950s to the 1970s provide striking confirmation of this reality.

On January 1, 1959, U.S.-backed dictator Fulgencio Batista fled Cuba in face of an advancing Rebel Army and of a spreading popular insurrection. The two-year-long revolutionary war waged by the Rebel Army under the command of Fidel Castro from its base in the Sierra Maestra mountains was over. The working people of Cuba in their millions took their future in hand. The first Free Territory of the Americas was born.

The popular victory over the dictatorship and the accelerating revolutionary transformation of Cuban society sounded a clarion call that echoed from Tierra del Fuego to the Río Bravo and beyond. Ordinary men and women of Cuba tenaciously and successfully resisted the fury of U.S. imperialism's reaction, demonstrating in practice, as the Second Declaration of Havana proclaimed, "that revolution is possible." Their actions won new generations of youth, determined to emulate what the Cuban people had done, and gave impetus to already deepening battles across the length and breadth of South America for land, national sovereignty, and against the brutalization of labor.

As Fidel Castro told a July 26, 1960, rally—held in the cradle of the revolution in the mountains of eastern Cuba—the revolution was making that country an "example that will convert the Andes into the Sierra Maestra of the American continent."

■

The Cuban Revolution, its staying power, and its weight in world politics can only be understood in the broad sweep of the twentieth and twenty-first centuries, astride which Cuba stands as the forward-most position established and held in the broadening national liberation struggles that accelerated following World War II.

Profound economic and social changes on the land and in the size and structure of the working class internationally were brought about by the global crisis of the Great Depression. International finance capital emerged from that crisis only with the help of the expansion of war-fueled production for the imperialist slaughter and the postwar reconstruction bonanza. These depression- and war-wrought changes in countryside and city the world over gave powerful impetus to anti-imperialist movements throughout colonial and semicolonial countries, from Indonesia, Vietnam, India, and Ireland, to the Mideast and virtually the entire continent of Africa, to the Americas.

This worldwide advance of national liberation battles found expression within the United States as well. A mass proletarian upsurge of Black Americans brought down the institutional racism of "Jim Crow" segregation, which had dominated the South since the defeat of the post–Civil War Radical Reconstruction and had reinforced discrimination and segregation throughout the country.

In Latin America, as Rodolfo Saldaña here describes, a 1952 revolutionary explosion in Bolivia was the high point of popular struggle in the years between the end of World War II and the victory in Cuba. With Bolivia's powerful tin miners in the front ranks, working people won sweeping concessions from imperialist interests and the country's ruling capitalist families. The upheaval resulted in nationalization of the largest mines, legalization of the trade unions, initiation of land reform, and elimination of the literacy requirement that had effectively disenfranchised the majority of Bolivia's people, the Aymará- and Quechua-speaking indigenous population. But Bolivia remained one of the poorest countries in the Americas; only Paraguay and Haiti had lower per capita incomes.

On July 26, 1953, little more than a year after the popular upsurge in Bolivia, the opening deed in the revolutionary struggle to overthrow the Batista dictatorship in Cuba was carried out. Some 160 youth under the leadership of Fidel Castro assaulted the Moncada garrison in Santiago de Cuba and another in nearby Bayamo.

Simultaneously, the young Argentine doctor Ernesto Guevara— later to become Che, one of the central leaders of the Cuban Revolution and commander of the 1966–67 revolutionary front in Bolivia discussed in this interview—was setting off on a political journey through the countries of Latin America. Drawn to Guatemala in 1954 as imperialism was organizing to overthrow the Jacobo Arbenz regime there, Guevara escaped to Mexico where he soon met the leaders of Cuba's newly formed July 26 Movement, recently released from Batista's prisons following a nationwide amnesty campaign. Guevara signed on as the troops' doctor and joined the *Granma* expedition that landed on the shores of eastern Cuba in December 1956 to launch the revolutionary war that culminated two years later in the overthrow of the U.S.-backed tyranny.

In Bolivia, Rodolfo Saldaña had dropped out of school and was starting work at Bolivia's largest tin mine, Siglo XX (Twentieth century) to build the Communist Party of Bolivia among the miners.

These interconnected threads are indispensable for understanding the events at the center of this book. By the mid-1960s, as Saldaña emphasizes, the class struggle in Bolivia, which had accelerated coming out of World War II, was once again reaching explosive dimensions. Political polarization was sharpening throughout the Southern Cone of Latin America. World politics was more and more dominated by U.S. imperialism's rapidly escalating war to crush the national liberation struggle of the Vietnamese people and the growing mass resistance to Washington's war within the United States and worldwide.

When Che Guevara, backed by Cuba's leadership, concluded that conditions were favorable to launch a revolutionary front in Bolivia, there was nothing casual or uninformed about the decision. Guevara's course was to establish a guerrilla front of internationalist volunteers that could regroup revolutionary forces throughout the region. Their goal was to forge a fighting anti-imperialist movement of workers, peasants, and youth that would overturn the military dictatorship in Bolivia that defended the landed, mining, and other capitalist interests in that country. In the process, they aimed to open the road to socialist revolution on the South American continent.

By October 1967, through the combined efforts of special U.S.-trained Bolivian army units and intelligence operations directed from Washington, Che's diminished troops had been cornered. The defeat of the revolutionary front was sealed by the annihilation of all but a handful of its remaining forces on October 8, including the wounding, capture, and execution of Guevara himself.

In the months and years that followed, a political debate raged among revolutionary-minded forces not only in Bolivia and Latin America, but around the world, assessing the reasons for the defeat. Many political forces who had opposed the revolutionary course of Cuba's leadership from the days of Moncada onward argued that the defeat of Che's *guerrilla* stemmed from a political misestimation by Guevara and the Cuban leadership. According to these voices, the workers and peasants of Bolivia were indifferent at best to the *guerrilla* initiative; conditions for a revolutionary course of struggle were lacking in Bolivia. Others claimed even more provocatively that Cuba's revolutionary leadership had abandoned Che and his forces and failed to take measures that could have reestablished contact with the guerrilla unit, rescuing the combatants from encirclement.

Rodolfo Saldaña's account, published here for the first time, makes a unique contribution. It comes from a Bolivian revolutionary who joined with Che Guevara in the 1966–68 campaign, and throughout a lifetime of political work remained true to the same course. Only *My Campaign with Che*, by the central Bolivian leader Inti Peredo, offers a similar firsthand account of the struggle from the perspectives of the Bolivian revolutionaries involved. Peredo's book, written shortly before he was killed in 1969 by the military dictatorship in La Paz, circulated in several countries of Latin America in the 1970s. It was translated and published for the first time in English in 1994 by Pathfinder Press together with a new translation of Guevara's *Bolivian Diary*.

Rodolfo Saldaña was a founding member of the ELN (the National Liberation Army) of Bolivia, the name taken by the forces under Che Guevara's command following their first military engagement with the armed forces of the Bolivian dictatorship in March 1967. A Central Committee member of the Communist Party of Bolivia, he broke with the party in 1966 over the refusal of the leadership under general secretary Mario Monje to collaborate with Che's effort.

Saldaña was slated to join Che's *guerrilla* as a combatant, but the responsibilities given him by Che, and the course of the guerrilla struggle itself, kept him at the head of the ELN's clandestine network in the cities and tin mining regions. He carried out the difficult and dangerous assignments of recruiting fighters among working people and youth, especially from the miners, and of providing logistical support for the guerrilla front. In his *Bolivian Diary*, Guevara noted that Saldaña "made a very good impression on me" when he visited the guerrilla camp at the beginning of the campaign.

Following the death of Guevara and most of the combatants, Saldaña helped organize the rescue and escape of the five survivors, three of them Cuban and two Bolivian. In the heat of the political battles that ensued, he worked to consolidate new forces in Bolivia and to relaunch the revolutionary struggle.

Of particular value in the account Saldaña gives here is the concrete, historical perspective he offers on the character of the class struggle in Bolivia and the long-gestating social, political, and economic realities that created the "fertile ground" for revolutionary struggle in the 1960s and '70s. In the process, he gives the lie to those who have argued that Che's *guerrilla* failed because it was a political adventure, ignorant of and alien to the conditions of Bolivia, and drew only an indifferent or hostile response from the country's workers, peasants, and youth.

Of value also is the picture he provides of the political and class trajectory of cadres of the Bolivian Communist Party such as himself and Rosendo García Maismán, the leader of the mine workers federation at Siglo XX. It comes as no surprise that they were among the small handful who broke with the party to chart a course, together with Che, towards the revolutionary struggle for power.

In passing, Saldaña also answers those who tried to use the defeat of the Bolivian front to slander the Cuban leadership for supposedly failing to provide necessary logistical support for Che and his comrades. He dismisses as simply uninformed— or nefarious—those who have sought to drive a wedge between Che and the revolution in Cuba he helped to lead, the revolution that made him the person he became.

In subsequent years Saldaña spoke little about his political experiences as part of the Bolivian vanguard that fought alongside Che. Of modest demeanor, he gave virtually no interviews. On the thirtieth anniversary of Che's death, while living and working in Havana, he provided invaluable help in the preparation, first in Spanish and then in English, of *Pombo: A Man of Che's 'guerrilla.'* That firsthand account by Harry Villegas (*Pombo*), a member of Che's general staff in Bolivia, was published by Editora

Política in 1996 and by Pathfinder Press in 1997. In the course of this work, Saldaña agreed to talk with Pathfinder editors Mary-Alice Waters and Michael Taber about Bolivia and the revolutionary campaign led by Guevara. The interview took place in Havana on April 26, 1997.

It was originally slated for publication in the fall of 1997 as part of the commemoration of the thirtieth anniversary of Guevara's death in combat. But Saldaña's health prevented him from reviewing the interview at the time. He completed his editorial work shortly before his death in June 2000.

■

Fertile Ground is being published simultaneously in Spanish by Editora Política and in English by Pathfinder Press. Iraida Aguirrechu, editor-in-chief of the current affairs department of Editora Política, the publishing house of the Central Committee of the Communist Party of Cuba, deserves special appreciation. Without her determined efforts the preparation of the interview for publication might never have been brought to completion. The support and encouragement of Brigadier General Harry Villegas was also decisive.

The extensive interview was transcribed by Mirta Vidal and translated by Michael Taber.

A number of photos of events in Bolivia and of Saldaña himself are published courtesy of Gladys Brizuela, Saldaña's companion of many years. Pedro Glasinovic, editor-in-chief of the daily *Presencia* in Bolivia, and Delfín Xiqués of *Granma* in Cuba also provided invaluable aid in searching for and providing photos of the class struggle in Bolivia.

Mary-Alice Waters
December 2000

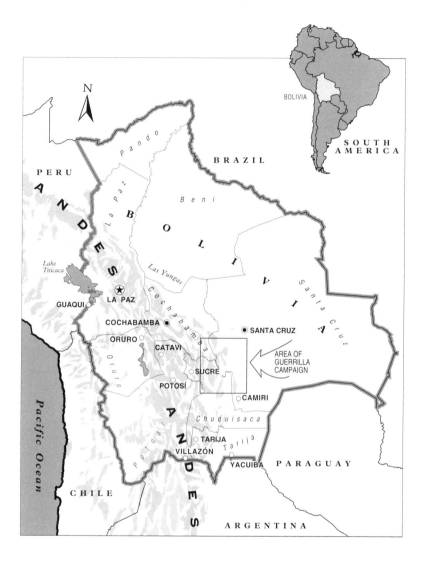

N

PERU

BRAZIL

BOLIVIA

SOUTH
AMERICA

Pando

La Paz

B
Beni

O
L

Las Yungas

I

Lake
Titicaca

Cochabamba

V
I

Santa Cruz

GUAQUI

LA PAZ

A

COCHABAMBA

ORURO

● SANTA CRUZ

CATAVI

Oruro

SUCRE

AREA OF
GUERRILLA
CAMPAIGN

POTOSÍ

A

CAMIRI

N

Chuquisaca

D

Potosí

TARIJA

E

VILLAZÓN

Tarija

S

YACUIBA

PARAGUAY

Pacific Ocean

CHILE

ARGENTINA

350 KILOMETERS

220 MILES

Bolivia

Chronology

1951

May — A right-wing military junta assumes power in Bolivia after annulling the results of the presidential election in which the Revolutionary Nationalist Movement (MNR) had won a plurality in the first round. The new junta carries out a wave of repression against the workers movement and adopts an "austerity" budget centered on meeting debt obligations to imperialist interests. Later that year, the U.S. government announces a steep cut in the price it will pay for Bolivia's tin. Following months of negotiations in which Wall Street and Washington refuse to budge, Bolivian miners launch a strike and street protests in late 1951 and early 1952.

1952

April 9 — Revolutionary upsurge, led by Bolivian trade union movement with tin miners in the vanguard, topples military government. A new regime is installed headed by Víctor Paz Estenssoro of the MNR. As byproducts of the powerful popular upsurge, the largest tin mines are nationalized, the trade unions are legalized, land reform is initiated, and Bolivia's indigenous majority are enfranchised.

1953

July 26 — Some 160 revolutionaries led by Fidel Castro launch insurrectionary attack on the Moncada army garrison in Santiago de Cuba and another in nearby Bayamo. The combatants fail to take the garrisons, and over 50 captured revolutionaries are murdered. Castro and 27 other fighters are subsequently captured, tried, and sentenced to up to 15 years in prison.

1954

March 1 — Four Puerto Rican Nationalists fire shots into the air in the U.S. House of Representatives in Washington, D.C., to draw attention to the Puerto Rican struggle for independence. They are imprisoned for over a quarter of a century.

June–September — Seeking to crush worker, peasant, and student struggles in Guatemala accompanied by limited land reform initiated by regime of Jacobo Arbenz, mercenary forces backed by the CIA invade the country to oust government. Among those volunteering to fight the attack organized by Washington is 26-year-old Argentine doctor Ernesto Guevara, drawn to Guatemala by the upsurge in struggle. Arbenz refuses to arm the population and resigns June 27; mercenary forces enter Guatemala City in August.

1955

May 15 — Following a nationwide amnesty campaign, Fidel Castro and the other imprisoned Moncadistas are released. Within several weeks the July 26 Revolutionary Movement is formed. In July Castro and other revolutionaries go to Mexico, where they prepare to relaunch the revolutionary armed struggle.

1956

July — Amid mounting anti-imperialist sentiment and actions in Egypt, government of Gamal Abdel Nasser nationalizes the largely British- and French-owned Suez Canal. Despite military assaults over the next four months by combined Israeli, French, and British forces, the Egyptian government refuses to back down and secures control of canal by November 1956.

December 2 — Eighty-two members of the July 26 Movement, including Fidel Castro, Raúl Castro, Che Guevara, and Juan Almeida, arrive in Cuba from Mexico aboard the yacht *Granma* to initiate the revolutionary war against Batista dictatorship. Rebel Army is born.

1957

September — In face of demands across the United States to enforce the 1954 Supreme Court decision barring racial segregation of schools, Central High School in Little Rock, Arkansas, admits nine Black students. As the governor of Arkansas unleashes racist mobs to assault Black youth, Washington responds to call by supporters of Black civil rights to send in federal troops to protect students and parents implementing the order.

1958

May — Demonstrations in Argentina, Paraguay, Bolivia, Peru, Venezuela, and other Latin American countries protest U.S. Vice President Richard Nixon's tour and denounce U.S. domination of Latin America.

1959

January 1 — Triumph of the Cuban Revolution. In the face of an advancing Rebel Army under the command of Fidel Castro and a popular insurrection led by the July 26 Movement, U.S.-backed dictator Fulgencio Batista is forced to flee.

March — With 24,000 tin miners on strike, street demonstrations by students throughout Bolivia denounce U.S. domination of the country. Workers and youth confront the increasingly corrupt and fractured MNR government.

May 17 — The Cuban revolution initiates a deep-going agrarian reform, confiscating the large landed estates of foreign and Cuban owners, and distributing land titles to hundreds of thousands of peasants.

November 1 — Some 2,000 Panamanian youths cross into Canal Zone to plant Panamanian flag there. Tear-gassing and assaults by club-wielding U.S. forces spark further protests by workers and students, demanding nullification of 1903 treaty imposed on Panama giving Washington perpetual control of the canal and Canal Zone.

1960

August 6 — In response to escalating U.S. economic aggression and sabotage, the revolutionary government in Cuba decrees the nationalization of major U.S. companies there. By October virtually all large-scale Cuban-owned industry is also nationalized.

1961

April 17–19 — First military defeat of U.S. imperialism in Latin America, as Cuban Revolutionary Armed Forces and popular militias, defending Cuba's socialist revolution, crush U.S.-organized mercenary invasion at Bay of Pigs.

1962

February 4 — Rally of one million in Havana's Plaza of the Revolution denounces U.S. imperialist economic embargo imposed earlier that week and proclaims the Second Declaration of Havana, underlining support for revolutionary struggle throughout the Americas.

July 3 — Following an eight-year national liberation struggle, Algerians win independence from France. A revolutionary government, led by Ahmed Ben Bella, soon comes to power, opening road to close political collaboration with Cuban government.

October 22–28 — Washington orders a naval blockade of Cuba and places U.S. armed forces on nuclear alert to demand removal from the island of a Soviet-supplied nuclear missile defense. The missiles had been installed following a mutual defense agreement between Cuba and the Soviet Union in face of Washington's renewed preparations to launch an invasion of Cuba. In response to U.S. aggression, millions of Cuban workers and farmers mobilize to defend the revolution, in effect saving the world from nuclear war. Following an exchange of communications between Washington and Moscow, Soviet premier Nikita Khrushchev, without consulting the Cuban government, announces his decision to remove the missiles.

1963

April–May — Black civil rights fighters in Birmingham, Alabama, conduct mass marches and sit-ins to desegregate public facilities. As they courageously defend themselves against brutal police assaults, the events become known as "The Battle of Birmingham."

May — An attempt to establish a guerrilla movement in Peru to overturn the pro-U.S. military dictatorship is crushed in Puerto Maldonado. Its leader Javier Heraud is killed.

May 29 — Peruvian revolutionary peasant leader Hugo Blanco is captured and jailed following several years of mass struggle by peasants for land in the valley of La Convención.

September — A guerrilla nucleus aimed at overthrowing the Argentine regime is established in the Salta mountains of northern Argentina, led by Jorge Ricardo Masetti, working closely with Che Guevara in Cuba. In collaboration with Guevara, logistics and support are coordinated from Bolivia by Cuban revolutionaries José María Martínez Tamayo and Abelardo Colomé Ibarra, as well as several members of the Bolivian Communist Party, including Rodolfo Saldaña.

1964

January 9 — U.S. troops kill some twenty Panamanians and wound hundreds during nationalist protests provoked by refusal of U.S. officials to fly Panamanian flag wherever U.S. flag is displayed. Over the following week, thousands mobilize to demand sovereignty over Panama Canal.

March–April — The guerrillas in the Salta mountains are crushed by Argentine military; Masetti is killed.

March 31–April 2 — A U.S.-backed military coup d'état in Brazil overthrows the government of João Goulart and inaugurates bloody reign of terror.

August — Following a naval incident manufactured by Washington in the waters off Indochina, the U.S. Congress passes the Gulf of Tonkin resolution. Bombing of North Vietnam and rapid escalation of the war begin. By 1969 there will be some 540,000 U.S. troops in Vietnam.

October — Nationwide struggles against the corrupt and unpopular MNR government sweep Bolivia's cities and countryside, with strikes, protest demonstrations, and street battles. Some 3,000 miners, many of them armed, battle the army on the plains of Sora Sora. More than fifty miners give their lives in the showdown. In the wake of the battle, numerous union leaders are arrested and union locals shut down.

November 4 — In the midst of the popular upsurge, a military coup is carried out by René Barrientos, Bolivia's vice president and head of the air force, and army commander Alfredo Ovando. Barrientos becomes president. Workers leaders arrested the previous month are released, and antiunion measures are lifted.

November 18 — Haydée Tamara Bunke *(Tania)* arrives in Bolivia from Cuba to begin intelligence work in preparation for initiating a guerrilla front to coincide with deepening popular struggles throughout South America's Southern Cone.

1965

February 21 — Malcolm X, internationalist leader of the revolutionary struggle for Black liberation and against U.S. imperialism, is assassinated in New York City.

April 1 — Che Guevara writes farewell letter resigning leadership responsibilities in Cuba's revolutionary government in order to participate in revolutionary struggles abroad. While awaiting preparation of preconditions to begin operations in the Southern Cone of South America, he goes to the Congo, where he heads a contingent of more than 100 Cuban volunteers giving assistance to popular forces fighting that country's pro-imperialist regime.

April 28 — Some 24,000 U.S. troops invade the Dominican Republic to crush a popular uprising against the Washington-backed military junta there.

May — Barrientos regime provokes confrontation with unions by lowering miners' wages and arresting large numbers of workers leaders, including Juan Lechín, head of the Bolivian Workers Federation (COB). Workers respond with a general strike and seizure of the tin mines. The regime intensifies repression, jailing more union leaders and forcing others into exile. The army sends troops to occupy the mining camps, killing many.

June 19 — Revolutionary Ben Bella government in Algeria is overthrown in military coup.

August — A rebellion by the Black community of Watts in Los Angeles drives the police out of the community. Some 13,000 National Guardsmen put down the uprising, leaving 36 dead, 900 injured, and 4,000 arrested. The Watts rebellion is first of numerous uprisings in Black communities of major U.S. cities over the subsequent three years.

October — A wave of strikes in Bolivia demands freeing of union leaders and restoration of wage levels, amid growing confrontations in the cities and mining areas.

October 3 — During a public meeting to introduce the Central Committee of the newly founded Communist Party of Cuba, Fidel Castro reads Guevara's letter of farewell.

October–November — Rodolfo Saldaña and Coco Peredo travel to Cuba, where they ask for military training. Responding to a request by the Bolivian Communist Party leadership, Cuba concurs.

1966

January 3–14 — Tricontinental Conference of Solidarity of the Peoples of Asia, Africa, and Latin America is held in Havana, attended by anti-imperialist fighters from around the world.

January — A number of Bolivian CP cadres and youth leaders, including Inti Peredo, Coco Peredo, Saldaña, Jorge *(Loro)* Vázquez, Benjamín Coronado, and Ñato Méndez begin military training in Cuba.

January 3 — Seven thousand copper miners in Chile go out on strike against a subsidiary of the U.S.-owned Kennecott Copper Corp. Workers at other copper mines wage sympathy strikes. Police murder of protesting miners in March leads to general strike call by Chilean workers federation. After Fidel Castro declares his solidarity with strikers, Chilean president Eduardo Frei accuses Cuba of being behind the strike wave.

March — Cuban internationalist José María Martínez Tamayo *(Papi, Ricardo)* arrives in Bolivia to organize preparations for a revolutionary guerrilla front to be centered in Peru or Bolivia.

June — Government of Argentine president Arturo Illía is overthrown in military coup led by General Juan Carlos Onganía. Military regime bans political parties and student organizations, while attempting a temporary accommodation with the trade union officialdom. By early 1967, however, the regime's refusal to make even minimal wage concessions provokes a round of strikes, which are met by police repression.

June 27 — Coco Peredo purchases a farm by the Ñancahuazú river in Bolivia as a possible site for training and support of the guerrilla movement.

July — Saldaña returns to Bolivia from Cuba.

With support of the revolutionary government, Che Guevara returns to Cuba clandestinely to supervise preparations for guerrilla front in Bolivia and training of Cuban volunteers.

July 25 — Cuban internationalists Harry Villegas (*Pombo*) and Carlos Coello *(Tuma)* arrive in Bolivia. Working together with José María Martínez Tamayo *(Papi, Ricardo)* and a number of Bolivian cadres, they help prepare for the guerrilla struggle.

September–October — Saldaña helps purchase two other farms in Caranavi as potential sites for the guerrilla camp.

November 7 — Arrival of Che Guevara at the Ñancahuazú camp in Bolivia.

November 20 — Saldaña visits guerrilla camp and meets with Guevara to work out logistical plans for the guerrilla unit.

December 31 — Bolivian CP leader Mario Monje comes to the Ñancahuazú camp and meets with Guevara. When his demand for leadership of the column is refused, he breaks off talks and urges Bolivian cadres to abandon the guerrilla unit—a course the central party leadership had in fact already decided a few months earlier.

1967

February — Saldaña goes to Siglo XX mine and meets with Rosendo García Maismán, the union's general secretary and a CP cadre, to seek the miners' support for the upcoming guerrilla struggle.

February–March — French writer Régis Debray and Argentine painter Ciro Bustos arrive at Ñancahuazú camp for discussions with Guevara on organizing international solidarity. Tania, who escorts them, remains with column when her jeep is discovered and her cover is blown.

March 23 — Guerrillas, in first combat action, ambush army troops along the Ñancahuazú. News of the action causes a sensation throughout the country. In response, Saldaña drafts a manifesto that is distributed in the cities and mines.

March 25 — The combatants adopt the name National Liberation Army of Bolivia (ELN).

April 11 — Bolivian dictatorship bans Communist Party, Communist Party (Marxist-Leninist), and the Trotskyist Revolutionary Workers Party (POR) and arrests a number of their leaders.

April 15 — 400,000 demonstrate against the Vietnam War in New York City and 75,000 in San Francisco.

April 16 — Guevara's "Message to the Tricontinental" is published in Cuba. Written in 1966 before he left Cuba for Bolivia, the message presents Guevara's assessment of the world struggle against imperialist oppression and capitalist exploitation. He calls for revolutionary forces everywhere to come to the aid of the Vietnamese national liberation movement and outlines perspectives for the struggle in Latin America.

April 17 — Main column commanded by Guevara in Bolivia heads south to escort Debray and Bustos to safety. The guerrillas' rear guard, led by Cuban commander Vilo Acuña *(Joaquín)*, remains behind to care for combatants who are sick. Meant to be apart three days, the two detachments remain permanently separated. The urban support network loses contact with both columns.

April 19–20 — Debray and Bustos are arrested. They are subsequently tried, convicted, and remain in jail until 1970.

May–June — Assemblies of tin miners at the Siglo XX mine vote to donate a day's pay to aid the guerrillas. Union leader Rosendo García Maismán organizes two groups of miners, one to join the guerrilla column, the other to carry out support tasks.

June — The Israeli regime launches simultaneous military assaults on Egypt, Jordan, and Syria. In the course of the six-day war, Israel seizes the Sinai Peninsula from Egypt, the West Bank from Jordan, and the Golan Heights from Syria. In response, the Palestinian national movement steps up struggle for Israeli withdrawal from all occupied Arab territories and the establishment of a democratic, secular Palestine.

June 23–24 — With resistance to the dictatorship's moves against tin miners growing, Bolivian army troops occupy mining camps at Siglo XX mines. In what becomes known as the Noche de San Juan massacre, troops open fire on workers and their families as they sleep, killing scores. García Maismán and others die putting up armed defense of union hall.

June 26 — A funeral for the victims of the Noche de San Juan massacre turns into a protest demonstration against the government by 30,000 miners and other working people.

July 31–August 10 — Organization of Latin American Solidarity (OLAS) conference is held in Havana; the conference proclaims support for guerrilla movements throughout Latin America; Guevara is elected honorary chair.

August 31 — Betrayed to the army by a peasant, the guerrilla detachment led by Vilo Acuña *(Joaquín)*—which had been separated from the main guerrilla unit led by Guevara for four months—is ambushed and annihilated while fording a river. Seven guerrillas are killed in the battle, and two more are subsequently captured and executed.

September 14 — Hundreds of suspected ELN collaborators are rounded up and imprisoned in La Paz, crippling the organization's urban underground.

October 8 — Guevara's column is surrounded. Guevara is wounded in battle and taken prisoner, together with two other guerrillas.

October 9 — After consulting with Washington, the Bolivian government orders the execution of Guevara and the other captured guerrillas.

1968

January — Fighters from Vietnam's National Liberation Front mount the Tet Offensive, taking the fight against the U.S. occupation army into the heart of South Vietnam's cities.

February 17 — Three surviving Cuban veterans of the guerrilla front cross from Bolivia into Chile, after months of eluding massive government effort to capture them. They arrive in Cuba March 6. The two Bolivian survivors, including Inti Peredo, remain to regroup the revolutionary forces.

April 4 — U.S. civil rights leader Martin Luther King is assassinated in Memphis, Tennessee. Black communities erupt in rebellions across United States.

May–June — Student protests in France against the Vietnam War are violently repressed by the government of President Charles de Gaulle. Students occupy universities around the country and barricade streets. As workers join antigovernment protests and a general strike paralyzes the country, a prerevolutionary situation develops in France. The image of Che Guevara is on posters and banners everywhere.

July 1 — Guevara's diary is published in Cuba. The diary had been seized and turned over to the Bolivian government when Guevara was captured. A copy was given to Washington. Microfilms of the captured diary were smuggled to Cuba. Publication by Cuba foils plans by the Bolivian military and Washington to exploit their theft of the document. The next day the authorized Cuban edition is published in English translation in the U.S., and a half dozen other translations are quickly prepared around the world.

August — Inti Peredo travels clandestinely to Cuba, where he helps plan resumption of the revolutionary struggle, together with all the surviving Cuban members of the guerrilla column and others. By early 1969 Saldaña also arrives in Cuba for further military training.

1969

April 27 — Barrientos is killed in a helicopter crash. Luis Adolfo Siles Salinas replaces him as president.

May — A general strike erupts in Rosario, Argentina's second-largest city, followed by a massive uprising in Córdoba, the third-largest city. The *Cordobazo* ushers in seven years of sharpening class struggle in Argentina. After workers movement fails repeatedly to resolve conflict in its interests, the officer corps organizes 1976 military coup. During infamous "dirty war" waged by dictatorship of Gen. Jorge Rafael Videla, over ten thousand Argentines are estimated killed or "disappeared."

September 9 — Inti Peredo is killed in La Paz by Bolivian police and army forces, tipped off by an informer.

September 26 — Siles Salinas is overthrown in a coup by Gen. Alfredo Ovando.

November 15 — 750,000 anti–Vietnam War protesters march in Washington and 250,000 in San Francisco.

1970

May — Following the U.S. invasion of Cambodia and the murder of antiwar protesters at Jackson State and Kent State universities, a massive student strike and occupation of schools sweeps the United States, involving over four million students. Demonstrations of tens of thousands occur in scores of cities across the country as opposition to U.S. government policy broadens.

May — Saldaña is arrested by forces of the Bolivian dictatorship.

July — 75 ELN members attempt to set up a new guerrilla front in Teoponte, north of La Paz, under the leadership of Chato Peredo, brother of Inti. In a commando action, they take several employees of a U.S.-gold mining company hostage. Within eight weeks, military offensive annihilates all but a handful of the guerrillas.

July 22 — Saldaña and nine other prisoners are released and flown to Chile, in exchange for release of the ELN's hostages. Saldaña obtains political asylum in Cuba.

August–September — Class struggle sharpens throughout Bolivia as workers and students press for concessions and a sector of the ruling class demands harsher repressive measures.

October 6–17 — General Ovando resigns presidency and turns power over to an ultrarightist military junta. In face of massive popular mobilizations to counter this takeover, the Bolivian army divides and Gen. Juan José Torres carries out a coup, displacing the rightists.

1971

January 10 — An attempted coup against the Torres regime is defeated by a massive popular mobilization. Thousands of armed miners arrive in La Paz.

February — Riding the wave of popular mobilization, a Popular Assembly, an incipient workers' parliament, is formed in Bolivia and takes up quarters in Bolivia's legislative chambers.

August 19–22 — Following months of wavering and indecision by the leadership of the Bolivian workers movement, right-wing military forces led by Hugo Banzer overthrow Torres government. A wave of murderous repression follows.

'Bolivia was fertile ground for revolutionary struggle'

INTERVIEW WITH RODOLFO SALDAÑA

Rodolfo Saldaña makes a point during interview, April 26, 1997.

The 1952 popular upsurge

QUESTION: Many who disagree with the revolutionary perspectives Che Guevara fought for argue that he and his fellow combatants were mistaken in going to Bolivia in 1966. Can you give us some background on the class struggle in Bolivia that shaped this decision?

SALDAÑA: The Bolivian people have a long history of struggle. There have been moments of really violent confrontations between the people and the repressive forces, though the two sides were not equal. More than once in the history of the country there have been true popular insurrections that toppled governments. There have also been massacres of miners, peasants, factory workers, and other working people in the cities, mainly La Paz.

Perhaps the defining moment of popular struggle was 1952. At that time a military junta ruled the country. As head of the police force, the minister of the interior conspired and launched a coup, but popular participation began changing the character of events, giving rise to a popular insurrection. For several days there were armed confrontations in the streets of La Paz, Oruro, and other cities, and the popular forces came out on top.

That's how the revolutionary process of April 1952 began, with the fall of the military junta that was governing the country and the rise of the Revolutionary Nationalist Movement (MNR). Wherever there was a confrontation, the popular masses defeated the military forces. For all intents and purposes, in those cities where there were confrontations the army came apart.

QUESTION: Why did workers, peasants, and others take to the streets in 1952? What led up to it?

SALDAÑA: Three issues were central: nationalization of the mines, land reform, and universal suffrage.

Nationalization of the tin mines was a demand the people had embraced for many years, and as a consequence of the revolutionary upheaval, the great mining companies were nationalized. There were three tin mining consortiums: Hochschild, Patiño, and Aramayo.[1] These were taken over to form the state mining sector.

Mining was the foundation of the economy because Bolivia was one of the largest producers of tin in the world. At certain times it has been the main producer, and at other times, it was second, but it has always been among the leading producers.

During the Second World War, for example, tin production was expanded and prices were low. The United States built up its stockpile. Increasingly these tin reserves were used as a weapon. The U.S. would simply announce that it was going to sell from its reserves ten thousand tons, seven thousand tons, or whatever, and the world market price would drop. After 1952, this was utilized as a political weapon of the United States to pressure the Bolivian government to respond to imperialist interests. The simple announcement that it was going to sell a certain quantity of this mineral precipitated a fall in the world market price. Even if they did not actually sell it.

In addition, the profits generated by mining always ended up outside the country; they were not reinvested in Bolivia. So people

1. Each of these three companies was owned by Bolivian capitalist families with strong links to imperialist interests. Each had also located its headquarters outside Bolivia: Patiño in the United States, Aramayo in Switzerland, and Hochschild in Chile. U.S. and British capital had substantial minority shareholdings in Patiño, which accounted for 43 percent of Bolivia's tin production.

became conscious of the need to bring about a change.

For example, in Potosí, Oruro, and other cities and departments where the heart of mining is located, where for dozens of years—and in the case of Potosí, hundreds of years—the mineral wealth had been exploited, the people nevertheless still obtained their drinking water as in the colonial era, which did not meet the needs of the population. Similarly, the electricity and housing situations were critical. Because of conditions like these, nationalization of the mines was a measure supported by the majority of the Bolivian people.

Agrarian reform was also a measure demanded by the majority. Prior to 1952, peasants struggling for a parcel of land were murdered or imprisoned by the large landowners for defending their rights against landlord oppression and exploitation.[2]

Because of this whole situation, the 1952 events culminated in these two fundamental measures: agrarian reform and nationalization of the large mining companies.

The third important measure was universal suffrage. The right to vote was previously restricted to persons who knew how to read and write. The majority of the Bolivian people were illiterate, and continue to be today. Clearly at that time there was greater illiteracy than now. But even today it is true. It is not enough to go to school for a year or two, the little rural or urban schoolhouse. It's true they may have learned to read and write a little, but owing to lack of use they again sink into illiteracy. The poorest sectors do not have access to the daily press. They are unable to buy a newspaper, a book, a magazine.

Steps to meet the popular demands around these three issues really filled the population with enthusiasm. They opened up perspectives for the development of the country, for the economic and social development of Bolivia.

---

2. In the Bolivian countryside before 1952, some 92 percent of all cultivated land was owned by 6 percent of landowners. Most peasants lived in virtual bondage to the landlords.

Within Latin America as a whole the revolutionary process of 1952 awakened great hope. People thought that a new type of society would be built in Bolivia, a more just society, with a better distribution of wealth, with possibilities for human development. But things didn't work out that way.

Revolutionary process stalled and reversed

Very early on, pressures to limit and reverse these revolutionary measures in Bolivia began to be felt. These came from the United States government primarily, from the large corporations, from international bodies. These forces brought great pressures to bear on the government and on the governing party.[3]

Measures necessary for deepening the revolutionary process were not taken by those in power. So, shortly after 1952, the people began fighting to advance these measures, and later still, to defend them.

For example, it took an excessively long time for the agrarian reform to be carried out. Peasants were told that the land belonged to those who work it, but in practice, there was no instrument for legal implementation of the act, meaning that peasants were not being given title to the land. That took place so slowly that it signaled the real possibility of a reversal, posing the question of annulment of the Agrarian Reform Law. In actual fact, after 1952 the peasants seized the land. The former owners did not return to the countryside. But the legal implementation established by the agrarian reform law was missing. The peasants who occupied the land had no property deeds to codify that the large landed estates belonged to them.

---

3. During this period, Washington was also leading an effort to topple the government of Guatemala and crush political and social struggles there accompanying a limited land reform initiated by the regime of Jacobo Arbenz. The Arbenz regime was overthrown in a CIA-backed operation in June 1954. Dictators throughout Latin America were being armed and supported by Washington—from Fulgencio Batista in Cuba and Alfredo Stroessner in Paraguay to Anastasio Somoza in Nicaragua.

This process dragged on for years. I don't know whether it has concluded even today. I don't know if all the peasants of that period, 1952, have yet received their deeds.

The peasants took up collections to send their leaders to the cities. Peasant leaders sat around in waiting rooms at the offices directing the agrarian reform. For weeks, months, they waited, only to return to their homes empty-handed. This went on for years. In order to survive in the city during these long waits, many of these peasant leaders worked as haulers, carrying huge loads. This whole generation of leaders did truly back-breaking work.

A similar regression took place in subsequent years with respect to the mines. There began to be talk about returning the mining companies to their former owners, of privatizing them, or closing them down as unprofitable.

The management of the Bolivian Mining Corporation (COMIBOL)—the state enterprise formed by the nationalized mines—was disastrous, and deliberately brought it to unsustainability.

The resources generated by COMIBOL were used by the various governments in power to meet their operating expenses. In some cases these were used for investments in other sectors. They also served as sources of corruption and illicit enrichment on the part of its directors.

On the other hand, there was no investment in new technology or machinery to improve production and lower costs. This led the mining industry to a critical situation. There were plenty of foreign advisers who charged millions for their work, without leading to the adoption of any positive measure for the nationalized mining industry.

In later years the army was reorganized, with the help of U.S. advisers and equipment. In 1952, as a result of the popular victory, the Military College was closed, the main garrisons shut their doors, and a large part of the military personnel was discharged. In the process of reorganizing the army, a select number of officers were reincorporated. Later, during the Barrientos regime that came to power in 1964, massive numbers of officers and top-ranking cadets were reincorporated with a higher rank than they had in 1952, when they were defeated by the people in arms.

In its first few years, the MNR government headed by Víctor Paz Estenssoro had the support of the mass of peasants and workers—miners, factory workers, railroad workers, and so on. But in the final years of the 1950s, and at the beginning of the 1960s, these sectors of the population began to see that things were not going as they should.

Many conquests won through constant battles by the workers were taken away. The elimination of the inexpensive grocery stores in the mines, which supplied basic products for working families at subsidized prices, meant a significant decrease in workers' purchasing power. Wages suffered a continual decline through inflation. Massive layoffs in the mines and other sectors began. These facts meant that confrontations with the government became more and more violent. After 1952 various governments succeeded each other belonging to the same ruling party, the MNR. Between 1960 and 1964 there were steadily deepening conflicts. The government's repression of the trade union movement, the workers movement, also became more and more violent. The year 1964 marked the high point of these confrontations.

In October 1964, on the plains of Sora Sora, near the city of Oruro, the largest armed conflict took place between the army and miners of Siglo XX[4] and Huanuni.

---

4. Siglo XX was the largest tin mine in Bolivia.

Revolutionary crisis in Southern Cone

QUESTION: Did the miners have their own militias?

SALDAÑA: Right after 1952 there were workers and peasants militias, which were armed. But over the years, in various ways, they were disarmed. If workers militias still existed, it was more or less in name only. But some workers, both in the cities and in the mining areas, kept their weapons. In the first years, after 1952, the peasants also purchased weapons, but little by little these were taken away.

At the end of October 1964, after the events of Sora Sora, there was a massive wave of arrests in La Paz of workers and students. I don't remember exactly, but it must have been much more than a thousand persons. This occurred at the end of October. But the struggle continued.

René Barrientos, general of the Bolivian air force and vice president of the republic at that time, organized a coup d'état on November 4, 1964. President Víctor Paz Estenssoro, the MNR leader who in 1952 had decreed the nationalization of the mines, the agrarian reform, and universal suffrage, was deposed. In the course of the coup there were armed confrontations with workers and others, in the streets of La Paz, for example. And there were even popular confrontations with the army itself, although the army adopted the stance that it was placing itself on the side of the people in carrying out the coup.

On November 4, 1964, workers seized a series of places, including the Panóptico jail in downtown La Paz. All the political prisoners there were set free, many of whom had been arrested

45

at the end of October. There were also union leaders who had been in jail for months. All these people went out into the streets.

A few days before, the government of Paz Estenssoro had closed the workers' radio stations. There were a number of these—certainly more than twenty—run by unions of miners, factory workers, railroad workers, construction workers, and others. All these radio stations were closed down. The union locals were closed. Their bank accounts, that is, the money the unions had in banks, or in company vaults, were frozen. The unions could not touch their money nor could they use their offices and meeting halls.

After November 4, Barrientos opened things up a little. The especially repressive measures against the workers were lifted. The workers' radio stations were permitted to resume. The union locals were reopened. But Barrientos soon faced growing working-class resistance to the dictatorial measures of his regime.

In May 1965 the government decreed a lowering of wages in the mines and ordered a massive wave of arrests of workers leaders. They were immediately deported, sending large numbers into exile in Argentina, Chile, and Paraguay. They were taken as far as possible from the Bolivian border—to the south of Argentina, to the south of Chile. Soon, little by little, they began to return to the country secretly.

In October 1965, the same year as the large-scale arrests, there were massive strikes by workers demanding freedom of their union leaders and the restoration of wage levels. The political movement was again heating up. There were armed confrontations in the main cities and mining centers.

In October, once again armed confrontations took place, and the military occupied the Central-Southern Council, a series of mines located in the south of the Department of Potosí, an area in which nothing had ever happened, that is, there had been no violent confrontations. The workers occupied other mines, too. So these armed confrontations in the cities themselves presented a new situation to us, to revolutionaries in Bolivia.

This was more or less the situation in the country at that time. We can thus answer the question of whether or not Bolivia was fertile ground for initiating the kind of revolutionary struggle Che envisioned.

QUESTION: What do you think?

SALDAÑA: I believe it was. The conditions existed.[5] There was repression; there were aspirations of the population that had not been satisfied and urgently required a solution; and the people could not fulfill their aspirations in the existing situation. There were solid reasons for the people to fight, to struggle, and they were increasingly doing so, but without results.

I also want to recall here the situation in Latin America as a whole. This was taking place in Bolivia in particular. But the same situation was being repeated, to different degrees, with its own characteristics, in the rest of Latin America. Guerrilla groups had arisen in a number of Latin American countries.

5. The preconditions for a revolutionary situation were summarized by Bolshevik leader V. I. Lenin in his 1920 pamphlet, *'Left-Wing' Communism—An Infantile Disorder:* "The fundamental law of revolution, which has been confirmed by all revolutions and especially by all three Russian revolutions in the twentieth century, is as follows: for a revolution to take place it is not enough for the exploited and oppressed masses to realise the impossibility of living in the old way, and demand changes; for a revolution to take place it is essential that the exploiters should not be able to live and rule in the old way. It is only when the 'lower classes' do not want to live in the old way and the 'upper classes' cannot carry on in the old way that the revolution can triumph. This truth can be expressed in other words: revolution is impossible without a nation-wide crisis (affecting both the exploited and the exploiters). It follows that, for a revolution to take place, it is essential, first, that a majority of the workers (or at least a majority of the class-conscious, thinking, and politically active workers) should fully realise that revolution is necessary, and that they should be prepared to die for it; second, that the ruling classes should be going through a governmental crisis, which draws even the most backward masses into politics (symptomatic of any genuine revolution is a rapid, tenfold and even hundredfold increase in the size of the working and oppressed masses—hitherto apathetic—who are capable of waging the political struggle), weakens the government, and makes it possible for the revolutionaries to rapidly overthrow it."

Military training

At that time, I belonged to the Communist Party, and as a member of the CP, my duty was to be wherever there was a struggle, wherever there was a fight. But we observed something: there was no structure, no order, no discipline. There was an amorphous mass that wished to fight, among whom we were working, but there was no discipline. At a certain moment some would go here and some would go there, with no military order. This convinced us of the necessity of acting in a truly organized manner, that is, with a military conception. So these events that Bolivia was living through convinced many Communist Party members of the need for us to receive military training, to have a military organization within the party capable of moving this situation forward.

The party's participation in that amorphous mass fighting in the streets was not enough. We needed a military structure above all. Revolutionaries were prepared to confront this task, together with our people, and for this we needed structure and training. Under these conditions, the party began to give in to pressure from some of us who wanted to prepare ourselves militarily.

This situation happened to coincide with the party's need for Coco Peredo[6] and me to travel to Cuba. When the possibility of the trip was raised with us, we saw it as an opportunity to arrange for the military training we had been discussing. So when we arrived in Cuba, this was the first thing we raised. But observing the mood, the willingness of members of the Communist Youth[7] who were studying here in Cuba, and recalling the willingness of many comrades in Bolivia with whom we had exchanged ideas, we rapidly saw the need to undertake more serious preparatory work.

In addition, the Tricontinental Conference, which was held at

---

6. Coco Peredo became a leading member of the guerrilla unit. He was killed in battle September 26, 1967.
7. The Communist Youth was the youth group of the Bolivian Communist Party.

the beginning of 1966, was fast approaching.[8]

I arrived in Havana at the end of October 1965 and Coco Peredo one or two weeks later. This was a few days after the events in my country that I mentioned—the confrontation at the Central-Southern Council. At the end of November or the beginning of December 1965, after he had been summoned by us, [CP general secretary Mario] Monje arrived in Havana.[9] We discussed with him the need for serious military training, on a broader scale. After hours of discussion and argument, in which Monje opposed this perspective, he changed his position and became enthusiastic about the ideas we were presenting.

Then Monje, as general secretary of the party, officially raised this with the appropriate bodies here in Cuba, and other comrades from Bolivia began to be summoned, among them Ñato Méndez, Loro Vázquez, and other comrades.[10] This was the group that began training. We're speaking now of 1966. At about the same time, a group of students belonging to the Communist Youth of Bolivia who were studying in Cuba was also undergoing training.

A second group that traveled to Cuba also began to receive training. This group included Inti Peredo, Benjamín Coronado,[11] and other comrades.

At the end of training, Monje selected the first group of four

8. The Conference of Solidarity of the Peoples of Asia, Africa, and Latin America—the Tricontinental—was held in Havana January 1966, attended by 430 delegates, representing anti-imperialist militants from 74 countries.

9. Monje had gone to Cuba prior to the Tricontinental conference. After it concluded in January 1966, he traveled to Moscow and then returned to Cuba, where he remained until May to receive military training together with other Bolivian CP members.

10. Ñato (Julio Méndez) and Loro (Jorge Vázquez Viaña) both joined the guerrillas. Méndez was killed November 15, 1967; Vázquez was captured in late April 1967 and murdered in army custody.

11. Inti Peredo was the leading Bolivian member of the guerrilla unit. His book, *My Campaign with Che,* is included as an appendix to the Pathfinder edition of the *Bolivian Diary.* Benjamín Coronado joined the guerrillas; he drowned in February 1967, before hostilities began.

comrades who were most trusted: Coco Peredo, Loro Vázquez, Ñato Méndez, and myself. Supposedly the four of us were to do work not specifically aimed at Bolivia, but related to the struggle on a continental scale.

Later, when he was back in Bolivia and had begun to vacillate, Monje would say that he had committed the party's support thinking that the struggle would not begin in Bolivia but somewhere else—that he hadn't known about what was planned. He did know about the continental character of the struggle, however, because already at that time he told us that our efforts would be geared along those lines. We were satisfied with that situation.

The guerrilla struggle begins

Argentina and Peru had originally been considered by Guevara to initiate the revolutionary struggle, but a series of defeats in those countries convinced him and his collaborators that Bolivia should be the starting point of their efforts, especially given the upsurge in that country in 1964–65.

One of the first decisions that had to be made was to pick an area that could serve as a rear training base. Three areas were considered: Caranavi, north of La Paz, in the Alto Beni region; Chapare, north of Cochabamba; and Santa Cruz, in southeastern Bolivia. Eventually a site was selected near Santa Cruz, on the Ñancahuazú river. A farm there was purchased on June 27, 1966, for use by the guerrilla combatants as an area for assembling and training the fighters. Subsequently, Saldaña was assigned to purchase another farm in Caranavi, although this one was never used.

■

We returned to Bolivia in July 1966. Monje had returned a little earlier.

After returning to La Paz, the four of us set to work; the object was preparation of a guerrilla front in Bolivia itself. We began to look for farms. I recall that on August 6, which is a national holiday, I first went to Monteagudo looking for a farm, later Muyupampa. And at the same time, Coco and Vázquez Viaña were traveling, also with the aim of looking for a place we could purchase as a base for receiving and training a group that would begin to act.

Shortly after this, Monje began to pull back. "They've deceived me, they told me this was for outside Bolivia," he said.

"And the farm we've purchased in Ñancahuazú?" I responded. "That was not for preparing something in Argentina, and you knew it. The Argentine border is very far from it. Had the aim been to enter Argentina, we would have gone to the border to be able to cross over to the other side. What you're raising now is simply not credible."

QUESTION: Over the last three decades, many critics of Che have claimed that his guerrilla nucleus in Bolivia had no prospects of success due to the backwardness of the Bolivian peasantry, that Che and his comrades misestimated the response their initiative would receive. What is your assessment of this?

SALDAÑA: One thing was clear to us at the time: the most politically developed parts of the countryside were the areas of colonization.[12] These were in the zone of Caranavi, that is, in the north of the department of La Paz, in the area of Las Yungas; in Chapare, in Cochabamba; and toward the north of Santa Cruz. These areas of settlement consisted of peasants from different regions and former workers—railroad workers, factory workers, miners—who in successive layoffs were left without work. As an alternative, a piece of land was offered them, of sizes ranging from ten to twenty hectares [25–50 acres] depending on the zone, to settle there and become peasants. These ex-workers had experience in union struggle, they knew how to organize, and they knew how to fight for their demands. Many also had political views. They were more politically developed than the average Bolivian peasant.

So these sectors of colonization were the areas of greatest

12. One of the provisions of the agrarian reform that came out of the 1952 revolutionary upsurge was to encourage landless peasants to settle on unclaimed land in sparsely populated regions of the country. This became known as colonization.

political development, both in the sense of receptivity, of understanding the reasons for the struggle, as well as being the most willing to join up. Because people there would see the *guerrilla* as the instrument capable of making their aspirations a reality.

We always kept this in mind, and with this aim we purchased two plots in the Caranavi zone—inward from Caranavi, very close to Puerto Linares, but in the documents about Che's guerrilla front it appears as Alto Beni or as Caranavi. We purchased these two plots of land in the name of Orlando Bazán—known as Camba—and Eusebio Tapia, who eventually became one of the rejects.[13] The two of them were placed there together with Papi[14] and Ñato Méndez, when we made the purchase. All this was in the latter half of 1966. They remained there, doing a few chores, living on those two plots.

QUESTION: So it wasn't unusual for people to settle on a plot of land that had already been colonized?

SALDAÑA: It was normal for someone who was established there for some time to transfer his plot to another person. The same office that registered the colonizers would then change the name. "So-and-so cedes his plot to so-and-so," and he keeps the person's debts. Based on the amount of time he stayed, there would be an adjustment for a certain amount of money as payment for the plot.

Together with Papi, I traveled to the zone, before and after I was to make the purchase. During the first trip, more or less, we noted the people who seemed to want to sell their lots, and we looked for two contiguous plots that had a fairly large strip of land.

QUESTION: What was the aim of the Ñancahuazú farm?

13. Four individuals were expelled from the guerrilla unit at the end of March 1967. They became known as the "rejects" and accompanied the guerrillas as they awaited the opportunity to be released.

14. Cuban combatant José María Martínez Tamayo. He had arrived in La Paz in March 1966 to coordinate preparations for the guerrilla effort. He was killed in combat July 30, 1967.

SALDAÑA: The farm was to be a base far from the area of guerrilla operations. It was to be a base of support, very far from the base of operations. As you can read in his diary, Che asked me to obtain an agronomist for the Ñancahuazú farm. That is, it was a farm that was to be worked normally, to produce.

Zone of operations

On April 17, 1967, the guerrilla unit split up, supposedly for only three days. Guevara led most of the combatants on a march that would enable French writer Régis Debray and Argentine painter Ciro Roberto Bustos to escape. These two individuals had been visiting the guerrilla base to discuss with Guevara plans for support work in their respective countries. But they were arrested soon after their departure, and after a widely publicized trial, were convicted and remained in prison until 1970. The two guerrilla detachments—one led by Guevara and another led by Joaquín (Cuban commander and internationalist volunteer Vilo Acuña)—were never reunited. On August 31 Joaquín's unit fell into an ambush.

■

An unanticipated situation came about, in which the guerrilla unit was permanently divided in two groups. This began as a temporary measure, meant to last a few days while Che got Debray and Bustos out of the zone. However, the two groups were unable to meet up again in the indicated time, and up to the end of August—which is when Joaquín's group was ambushed and annihilated—this whole time was spent in search of the other group, seeking to meet up again.

The area that the guerrilla unit was compelled to operate in has a very low population density. Bolivia has about 1,100,000 square kilometers [424,000 square miles]. At the time, it had around five million inhabitants, the majority of them concentrated in the area of the Altiplano and the valleys. There are areas in which there is less than one inhabitant per square kilometer. It was a very unpopulated area. In addition, it is a very isolated region, without political development. It was clear to us that other zones had greater possibilities for recruitment, for obtaining support. But they were compelled to stay in that region, which was not the best, not the most propitious, in order to try to reunite the two groups.

When the existence of the guerrillas became known, after the first battles, we contacted peasants from a few regions of the Altiplano—from the valleys and areas of colonization. They agreed to join up with the guerrilla unit and were seeking ways of doing so.

These are things that must be considered when making an evaluation, when speaking about the results.

Role of Communist Party

QUESTION: What was the role of the Bolivian Communist Party as the conflict sharpened?

SALDAÑA: In October 1966, more or less, the leadership of the CP decided not to participate in the revolutionary front Che was organizing. Monje, utilizing false and tendentious information, sowed confusion among some members of the Secretariat and Political Commission and got them to withdraw the party's support and participation. But this decision was not made official until December 31, when Monje came to the Ñancahuazú camp to meet with Che.[15]

There, with Che's authorization, Monje met with the Bolivians who were part of the guerrilla unit and told them that the party was not joining the struggle. He called on them to abandon it. No one followed Monje; he left the camp by himself. All the combatants expressed their determination to continue. Nevertheless, the decision of the party leadership meant we could not work in the cities with the members. Our work was very clandestine, very restricted. We dealt only with individuals we

15. That meeting ended in an open break between Guevara and the Bolivian CP, when Che refused to accede to the demand that Monje assume command over the guerrilla unit.

were absolutely sure of—those capable of deciding: "Yes, I'll join," knowing that the party would not participate, and what had earlier been a possibility was now a reality.

The party leadership, for its part, began to warn the membership that a new factional group had arisen, and that the party had to be prepared to confront it. They did so without saying what this new group supposedly out to split the party consisted of, or who was participating in this new effort. This campaign within the party escalated following December 31.

In February 1967 Jorge Kolle and Simón Reyes went to Cuba to discuss the situation.[16] Informed of the reality, they said the party had functioned that way because Monje gave the party leadership incorrect information. Kolle and Reyes made a commitment to correct the stance the party had assumed toward the guerrilla campaign.

They recognized that Monje had confused the party leadership. Then Reyes and Kolle said, "We're going to give our support." By the time they returned to Bolivia, the first battle had already taken place. Kolle told me, "The party will participate. I myself am willing to go."

And in practice this led to a commitment. We were put in contact with some party members who expressed a desire to join, and with other people who were also approaching the party with the same aim. Therefore, I believe there was a clash of different, contradictory positions within the party.

I was the first one to arrive at the camp after Che had come. I brought San Luis and Marcos[17] with me. I talked with Che about the party's stance. This was around November 20. We knew that the party was not participating due to Monje's actions and that we were facing the party's opposition. Che clearly stated

16. Jorge Kolle and Simón Reyes were members of the Bolivian CP's Central Committee Secretariat who visited Havana in February 1967. Kolle replaced Monje as CP general secretary in December 1967.

17. *San Luis* (Eliseo Reyes or *Rolando*) and *Marcos* (Antonio Sánchez) were members of the Central Committee of the Communist Party of Cuba who volunteered as combatants in Bolivia. Both were killed in battle.

Workers run toward an arsenal to obtain weapons during popular insurrection in La Paz, Bolivia, April 1952.

"Perhaps the defining moment of popular struggle was the insurrection of 1952. The revolutionary process awakened great hope. People thought that a new type of society would be built, a more just society, with a better distribution of wealth, with possibilities for human development. But things didn't work out that way."

AP/WIDE WORLD PHOTOS

GRANMA

"In its first few years, the MNR government had the support of the mass of peasants and workers. But in the final years of the 1950s, and at the beginning of the 1960s, these sectors of the population began to see that things were not going as they should. Between 1960 and 1964, there were steadily deepening conflicts. The year 1964 marked the high point of these confrontations."

Top left, women textile workers take to streets in La Paz, June 10, 1961. **Bottom left,** demonstrators march beneath banner of Bolivian Workers Federation (COB) in defense of the Cuban Revolution, early 1960s. **Top right,** popular demonstration confronts government forces in La Paz, October 30, 1964. **Bottom right,** President Víctor Paz Estenssoro (left) with General René Barrientos, March 1964, after Barrientos had been selected to run for vice president with Paz on the MNR ticket. In November Barrientos ousted Paz in a coup.

"Our struggle was taking place in Bolivia. But the same situation was being repeated, to different degrees, each with its own characteristics, in the rest of Latin America. Guerrilla groups had arisen in a number of countries."

Above, peasants in Peru demonstrate for "land or death," early 1960s. **Top right,** Ernesto Che Guevara addressing meeting of the Organization of American States (OAS) in Punta del Este, Uruguay, August 1961. The meeting, which rubber-stamped the Kennedy administration's proposal for an "Alliance for Progress," was designed by Washington to line up Latin American regimes against the Cuban Revolution. **Middle right,** Jorge Ricardo Masetti in the Salta mountains of northern Argentina, where he headed a guerrilla front, 1963–64. Saldaña worked on logistical support for the effort, as he did with a guerrilla movement in Peru.

Right, delegates from revolutionary organizations throughout the Americas hear Fidel Castro address the Organization of Latin American Solidarity (OLAS) conference in Havana, August 1967. The slogan, taken from the Second Declaration of Havana, reads, "The duty of every revolutionary is to make the revolution."

"News of the guerrilla front stirred the people as a whole. It had an impact on the class struggle in the entire country."

Above, students confront police August 1967, during antigovernment protest in La Paz. **Upper right,** members of the guerrilla unit at the Ñancahuazú camp; Inti Peredo is at left. **Middle,** Ernesto Che Guevara and Rodolfo Saldaña at the Ñancahuazú camp, November 20, 1966. **Bottom right,** the guerrilla unit fording a river in Bolivia, 1967.

"The support received from the miners gives the lie to charges that the Bolivian workers and peasants were indifferent to the struggle Che initiated."

Following the defeat of the guerrilla front led by Guevara, miners continued in the vanguard of struggles, which culminated in the mass working-class upsurge of 1970–71. **Top,** workers at the Siglo XX tin mine protest the right-wing coup led by Hugo Banzer in August 1971. Seen in the photo, at right, is a statue of a helmeted miner holding a rifle, commemorating the 1952 revolutionary upsurge. **Bottom,** miners protest Washington's attempt to drive down tin prices by selling off part of U.S. strategic reserves, June 16, 1973.

his opinion, his decision, that one must exhaust all efforts to do everything possible—and I also felt this way—to obtain the party's commitment to participate.

QUESTION: Che told you this in Ñancahuazú?

SALDAÑA: Yes. This was independent of whether or not the party would really change its stance. We foresaw that the best militants of the party, the true revolutionaries, would take the step forward, that is, that they would join the *guerrilla*. I believed that the same thing would occur with members of other political forces and other individuals. That was my view. And that's in fact what happened.

QUESTION: Did you remain members of the party?

SALDAÑA: No. By then, we weren't. We were members of the ELN [National Liberation Army]. We were not members of the party.

QUESTION: When did you cease considering yourselves members of the party?

SALDAÑA: More or less in October, at the end of October 1966.

I said earlier that in Cuba, Coco, Ñato, Vázquez Viana, and I had already made the commitment together with Monje, the five of us, of going ahead with or without the party. In other words, we were determined to go ahead. When Monje and the party leadership began vacillating, we were convinced that we had to go forward without them if necessary. That's why after talking with us, Che wrote in his diary on the first day that Bigotes[18] would collaborate regardless of the party's stance. "Rodolfo feels the same way." This sentence appears on the first page of his diary. And when I went to meet with him, the thing

18. Another nom de guerre of Jorge *(Loro)* Vázquez Viana. In his diary entry for November 7, 1966, Guevara noted, "Bigotes states he is prepared to collaborate with us whatever the party might do, but he is loyal to Monje, whom he respects and seems to like. According to him, Rodolfo feels the same way, as does Coco, but it is necessary to try to get the party to join the struggle. I asked him to help us, and requested he not inform the party until Monje—who is on his way to Bulgaria—arrives. He agreed to both things." *The Bolivian Diary of Ernesto Che Guevara* (Pathfinder, 1994), p. 78.

was even clearer, superclear. And that's why we spoke clearly with Che about the participation or nonparticipation of the party. We were speaking about a force different from our own. We wanted it to participate. That was the situation.

Although they threatened to expel a number of comrades in the leadership of the CP's youth organization, as well as other comrades, this step was never taken. Had they done so, there would have been a veritable storm in the party, because we were all among the most active members. The party leadership seemed to be playing a double game with us: to get us out of the way, while not expelling us and leaving open the possibility of taking credit if we succeeded.

Miners, students respond

QUESTION: What was the popular response within Bolivia on learning of Che's *guerrilla?*

SALDAÑA: After the first clash between the army and Che's forces occurred on March 23, I drafted a manifesto, and we distributed it in the cities. We did not yet have a name, so we were posed with the decision of what name the organization should use to address the people. We knew the decision rested with Che and the guerrilla group. That was where our command was. But we needed to say something to the people in some way, to explain somehow what was happening.

This was the document we used to begin to work in the mines, with which we began to work in the city, explaining more or less what the guerrilla struggle meant.[19]

QUESTION: Without mentioning Che?

SALDAÑA: Correct. Under those conditions, we had to do our work without mentioning Che. The enemy already knew there were guerrillas, and it had to have known that groups were working to support the guerrillas. We were telling them nothing they didn't know. There were individuals among the people, among the workers, however, seeking ways to make contact with the guerrillas, seeking that possibility. These were the reasons for what we did, and the conditions under which we did it.

QUESTION: What was happening among the tin miners?

19. The authorship of this manifesto was previously unknown; some attributed it to Guevara.

59

SALDAÑA: The support received from the miners is one of the things that gives the lie to charges that the Bolivian workers and peasants were indifferent to the struggle Che initiated.

I had been a miner at Siglo XX. I built the Communist Party there in the 1950s. So I knew the party members, many of whom I had recruited.

I went to Siglo XX, it must have been in February 1967. I spoke with Rosendo García Maismán, who in those days was general secretary of the union, of the miners of Siglo XX, and a leader of the party there. He was an intelligent comrade, a very capable and courageous comrade. Without entering into details, I informed him that a decision had to be made soon. Later, after the first battle, he and I met on a number of occasions. By then he was already one of us, and he began to form two groups. One of these groups was to join the guerrilla column, and the other was to carry out support tasks.

As to the miners' commitment to the struggle, we have the testimony of Rosendo García's widow in the film "Coraje del Pueblo" [Courage of the people]. This film seeks to reconstruct all the events of the Noche de San Juan massacre. There the widow of Rosendo García is interviewed, and she mentions the trip I made to Siglo XX to talk with her husband. The communiqué we spoke about earlier had been sent to Siglo XX for distribution. That task had already been carried out by the compañeros grouped around García.

The miners registered their support to the guerrillas at general assemblies. They decided that each worker would donate one day's pay to help the guerrillas. Their commitment shows us that there was generalized support among the workers. It's possible, of course, that there were some who were not in agreement. But the miners unanimously made this decision at their assembly.

QUESTION: This was in May or June?

SALDAÑA: This was at the end of May or at the beginning of June.

On June 24 there was supposed to be an expanded meeting

of the miners federation, that is, union leaders from all the country's mines were coming to Siglo XX. Representatives of the teachers and university students were also coming. In addition, this meeting at Siglo XX was to serve as a vehicle to discuss some general questions dealing with the workers' demands, and certainly it would have taken up support to the guerrillas.

During the night of June 23 into the dawn hours on June 24, the army entered the mining camp shooting, throwing grenades at the homes of the miners while they slept. This is why many women and children were among those killed. That was the Noche de San Juan massacre. The only place the troops encountered armed resistance was at the union hall, where Rosendo García was, together with the few who were able to respond to the call of the mine's siren. The union's siren would be sounded in the mornings so the workers would get to work; it's like an alarm clock. But the siren was also used to summon people to assemblies and as a warning about some danger. That night the siren was sounded.

Immediately the workers knew—since it wasn't time to go to work it had to be something else, some emergency, or an assembly. Something was happening.

With a few rifles, they confronted the army. A number of people were killed there at the union hall, including Rosendo García Maismán, the central leader of the workers at Siglo XX. Many others died in their homes from machine-gun fire.[20]

The delegates who had arrived for the meeting hid out in the mines, and later in different ways they secretly left the area, which was occupied by the army.

This was the highest expression of support the guerrillas received, but this doesn't mean it was the only one. There were other demonstrations of support, although none reached this

---

20. Dozens were killed in the Noche de San Juan massacre. Guevara's response is contained in the ELN's Communiqué no. 5, "To the Miners of Bolivia," published by Pathfinder in *Pombo: A Man of Che's guerrilla* and in Guevara's *Bolivian Diary*.

level. There was a willingness among members of many political parties to join up. There was the attitude of many intellectuals. Proof of this can be found in poems written at the time the guerrilla struggle began, and after Che's death.[21] We collected these poems together in a book. And there were surely many others that were never compiled for inclusion, that remained anonymous. There were also songs. In short, there were a whole series of manifestations of support.

This is in response to those who say there was no support among the Bolivian people, that Che was isolated. That is not true. The guerrilla events after March 23 stirred the people as a whole, the population as a whole, in all their different social layers.

Support work in city

QUESTION: A biographical detail. You worked in the city all this time. What were you doing during this period?

SALDAÑA: I was supposed to join the guerrilla front as a combatant. That is what I had trained for. But there were a series of tasks to be carried out in the city, among them organizing the urban apparatus for logistical support, for recruiting combatants, and for other tasks. Secondly, we had the situation with the Communist Party.

In the first days of January, a few days after Monje's open break, he sought me out and told me about his discussions with Che. Monje explained his political view that a "foreigner" couldn't be at the head of the revolutionary forces in Bolivia, and that it would have to be the party—that is, him. Among his arguments was, "Not even Lenin could come here and seek to

---

21. On October 14, 1967, at a meeting of students at the University of Cochabamba proclaiming Che a "Bolivian patriot and citizen," Ramiro Barrenechea Zambrana read his poem, "To the Commander of the Americas." These and other poems are collected in a book edited by Barrenechea entitled *El Che en la poesía boliviana* [Che in Bolivian poetry] (La Paz: Caminos Editores, 1995).

lead us. It has to be led by us Bolivians."

I became indignant over this. I said that according to this view, we should renounce the name of our own country, because Bolivia is named after Simón Bolívar, a native of Caracas whose liberation army marched from one end of the American continent to the other. And likewise Sucre, our political capital, is named in honor of Antonio José de Sucre, the other Venezuelan military leader of Bolívar's expedition, which brought freedom to half the continent. That's when I broke definitively with Monje.

During this whole period of preparation, with the participation of the party, we had been able to put together an urban network. We had people working on different tasks of support to the guerrillas. When we no longer had the party's participation, we had to go looking for one comrade after the other.

Regarding those closest to us, we knew what they thought. We trusted in their honesty, their integrity—because in underground work, you don't just need good people; you need people capable of dying for a cause, capable of defending the cause. In case of arrest, a prisoner who turns informer is as harmful as a traitor, as an agent, because he can lead to the organization being broken up.

This is what we needed from militants in this work. It couldn't be otherwise. We needed militants who would defend the organization until death, knowing they were dying in battle, that they were not going to see the objective for which we're all fighting, but that their silence would assure the process continued. In no case is someone fighting to save his own life. He is struggling for the goals of us all.

It was difficult to assemble revolutionaries with this quality. Those closest to us, those we knew, those with whom we had been through years of struggle, were from the CP. They couldn't come from any other party, because we didn't even have friendships outside the organization. We knew a few other people, but our fundamental source was the party, and it was now difficult for us to work there.

We obtained García Maismán's commitment to join us. It was his union local that proclaimed its support in a general assembly. And a union leader cannot impose a measure of this nature, a *commitment* of this nature. It was the workers at their general assembly, undoubtedly with the information given them and so forth, who got their leader to adopt this determined stance. It was not just one person, it was thousands of workers in that assembly who decided this.

This is what we were involved in, trying to fulfill these and other tasks. The first battle had still not taken place and we were trying to find an agronomist, someone who knew something about agriculture and could run a farm. Where were we going to find such a person? We couldn't put an ad in the newspaper saying, "Agronomist wanted." We needed someone knowledgeable about farming who was a revolutionary, someone who would carry out this task, and who also knew there were risks in it. In other words, we needed a person who knew what we were doing. And we didn't have such a person at the moment. We knew a few trained agronomists, but they were members of the party. The party's withdrawal therefore made it more difficult for us to continue.

The comrades who arrived at the camp in the first days of January came with lists of Bolivians, saying, "Find this person, look for that person." They gave us lists of people who might be able to work with us, and we were combing over these possibilities, having meetings with these people.

On top of this, Tania decided on her journey. All this postponed my going, and eventually events trapped Tania inside the guerrilla front.[22] What did she do? Together with Debray and Bustos, she went to meet with Che and depart again, but Che's return to the main camp was delayed and the meeting

22. *Tania* (Haydée Tamara Bunke) was an Argentine-German who had lived in Cuba for several years. On Guevara's instructions, she had been stationed in Bolivia since 1964, where she had various intelligence and support responsibilities. In February 1967 she brought Argentine painter Ciro Roberto Bustos and the French writer Régis Debray to the guerrilla

got postponed. After the first battle her cover was blown. That was the situation.

When this situation came about, I was involved with the tasks of urban work, at the same time as I was recruiting people to go to the mountains. I was ready to go to the mountains with some other people; we had succeeded in acquiring weapons and a few other things. We were looking for the possibility of making contact. I was waiting for the moment to go, not just by myself but with other people.

camp for discussions with Guevara on support work in their respective countries. The beginning of combat caught Tania, Debray, and Bustos among the guerrillas, and the authorities were able to determine her identity after her jeep was found and traced to her, destroying years of work.

Rodolfo Saldaña, April 8, 1969, during military training in Cuba, in preparation for relaunching the revolutionary guerrilla struggle.

Trying to reestablish contact

One of the key tasks facing supporters of the ELN in Bolivia was to maintain contact with those in Cuba who were helping to coordinate logistics. As military operations developed, however, this task became more difficult and dangerous. Furthermore, it became more and more difficult for the urban network in La Paz and other cities to maintain contact with Guevara and his comrades in the zone of combat operations. By mid-April they had lost contact altogether.

■

We began to look for contact with Cuba, and the only possibility we had was through Chile.

I sent various persons to Chile, to try to make contact, and it was Estanislao Villca[23] who carried a message I wrote. In it I suggested—given the impossibility of making contact with Che—opening up a new front, to ease the pressure on Ñancahuazú. We already had weapons for this. We had even brought them to Caranavi and buried them at the farm of Estanislao Villca's father, with the intention of opening up a new guerrilla front.

Our concern was that since it wasn't possible to make contact with Che, we had to do something.

But the instruction from Cuba was not to do so, to try in-

23. Bolivian revolutionary Estanislao Villca was a member of the ELN. He later helped guide the three surviving Cuban guerrilla veterans through the military's encirclement and traveled to Cuba with them.

stead, in any way possible, to make contact with Che. That was the response we received. The goal, we were told, was to reinforce the main nucleus. Not to disperse forces but to concentrate them.

We had one comrade who was able to receive messages from Cuba. But his cover was blown very early on, because he had once helped the Peruvian survivors of Puerto Maldonado[24] return to Bolivia. Guerrilla activity had hardly begun when the police began looking for him. And Sánchez,[25] the Peruvian who was in Bolivia, was also being sought by the police, and we had to take him out of circulation. So the possibility of receiving communications from Cuba through him was closed off. We were thus left without the possibility of either sending or receiving messages, and that was why we looked to establish contact through Chile.

Later, a Japanese woman arrived in Bolivia from Cuba to get in touch with us. This was an indication of the desperation in Cuba to reestablish contact.

There were also other forms of contact. There was a Danish journalist who was able to get in touch with some of our people.

Soon another journalist approached us. The OLAS meeting was then being held.[26] We sent a tape recording to the OLAS meeting.

QUESTION: You sent a tape, by way of a Cuban contact?

SALDAÑA: Yes. Friends of Cuba, working for magazines and

24. In 1963 Peruvian revolutionaries seeking to set up a guerrilla nucleus were ambushed in Puerto Maldonado, Peru. The revolutionaries had entered through Bolivia, and the survivors escaped back over the border, aided by members of the Bolivian Communist Party.

25. *Sánchez* (Julio Dagnino Pacheco) was a Peruvian revolutionary living in La Paz, and a key member of the guerrillas' urban support network. Later, after being taken prisoner, he supplied valuable information to the repressive forces.

26. The Organization of Latin American Solidarity (OLAS) held its first conference in Havana from July 31 until August 10, 1967, proclaiming support to revolutionary movements throughout the continent. Guevara was elected honorary chair and "Latin American citizen of honor." The conference approved a "resolution of support to the struggle of the Bolivian guerrillas" and a message of greetings addressed to Che Guevara.

so forth, had access to Bolivia, but they also had the additional mission of seeking out contact with us. And those two journalists succeeded in reaching us. We gave one of them a tape.

This showed the desire to make contact, in different ways. So what some have charged about Cuba not understanding, forgetting about us, or not giving assistance is totally false.

Cuba did not abandon us

In addition, when it was learned in Cuba that the armed struggle had begun, Bolivians in Cuba and other countries began to assemble and receive training. There were people who went to Cuba from Europe, from the Soviet Union, from Poland, from different countries, to help us. And there were others who went directly to Bolivia.

All these things were done. In other words, Cuba did not abandon us.

Other fantasies have been raised by some people. For example, on October 8, 1992, when I was in La Paz, at a meeting at someone's house, some people asked, "Why didn't Cuba rescue Che? Why didn't they send a plane?" There are people incapable of understanding that some things can be done, and some things can't be done. There are things that are not real. There are things that come from someone's imagination. In one's imagination, I can take off and leave our planetary system and roam around who-knows-where, in the infinity of space. But that's not possible in reality, at least not at the present time.

Bolivia through 1971

In the four years after Che and his comrades fell in battle, Bolivia was rocked by momentous class battles. Dictator René Barrientos was killed in a helicopter crash in April 1969. His successor, Luis Adolfo Siles Salinas, was overthrown in a coup by Alfredo Ovando, the army chief of staff, in September. Under pressure from intensifying popular struggles, Ovando's regime adopted measures opposed by the bour-

geois and military forces most closely allied with U.S. interests. These forces organized a coup to oust Ovando in October 1970. Bolivian workers took to the streets and defeated the coup attempt. Juan José Torres, another officer, assumed power. A second attempted right-wing coup in January 1971 was also defeated through the mobilization of the toilers. Riding the wave of these mass mobilizations, Bolivian working people formed a Popular Assembly, an incipient workers parliament, in February. Following months of wavering and indecision by workers leaders, military forces led by Hugo Banzer overthrew the Torres government in August 1971 and unleashed a wave of murderous repression.

■

After Barrientos died, there was a very short transitional period where Siles Salinas was president—previously he had been the vice president, and then there was the government headed by Ovando.

The Ovando government nationalized Gulf Oil, which not long before had begun operations in Bolivia.[27] A whole series of U.S. imperialism's organs, like the Peace Corps, were thrown out of the country. Some of the CIA's operations were dismantled, like its phone-tapping center in La Paz. The U.S. military mission, which had its base in the area and was known as "little Guantánamo,"[28] was shut down in this period.

My view at the time was that the measures being adopted by the Ovando government did not have the unanimous support of the state apparatus, including the armed forces. While some elements were pushing to take another road, the apparatus of Barrientos was still intact. I predicted that the government's days were numbered. In addition, there was the weight of the

27. Under the Barrientos regime, Gulf Oil's share of Bolivia's oil production rose from 3 percent in 1964 to 82 percent in 1967.

28. The U.S. naval base at Guantánamo Bay in southeastern Cuba has been occupied against the wishes of the Cuban people since the beginning of the twentieth century.

United States rulers, who were decisive in Bolivia's situation; they could not be in agreement with Ovando's course.

So first they kicked some of the ministers out, and after that the government of Ovando went. Later, Juan José Torres came to power. Torres had been removed from command of the army. He was appointed president amidst a great popular upsurge, supported by a large majority of workers and peasants and others, plus a sector of the military. And he remained in power for one year, until the coup d'état in 1971, when Banzer assumed power.

Looking at the governments of Ovando and of Torres shows us to what extent the guerrilla effort had an impact on the class struggle in the entire country, including affecting the armed forces itself.

PHOTOS: HOY

Top, crowd outside La Paz prison July 22, 1970, awaiting release of Rodolfo Saldaña and nine other political prisoners. **Bottom,** Saldaña boarding a plane following his release.

The making of a revolutionary

QUESTION: Tell us something about your personal history. How did you become involved in political activity?

SALDAÑA: Well, my first political struggles began when I entered high school. I was always on the side of the revolutionary forces.

QUESTION: What year was this?

SALDAÑA: In 1947 I began high school in the city of Sucre. In 1946 there was a popular insurrection against the government of Villarroel. Villarroel was hanged from a lamppost in La Paz, together with one of his followers.[29]

QUESTION: What was the nature of his regime?

SALDAÑA: Villarroel was a military man. His government was considered connected to Argentina, sympathetic to Germany in the Second World War. He was also accused of being tied to Getulio Vargas in Brazil.[30] His government tried to take advantage of the interimperialist conflict in the international arena. So there was some connection to the Brazilian government in the era of the Second World War, some connection to Germany. At the same time, there was, to a certain degree, an easing of U.S. pressure, to try to keep the country on its side.

This was the period of the antifascist popular fronts, and the

---

29. Bolivia's president during the latter part of World War II, Gualberto Villarroel was hanged by a crowd in front of the presidential palace in La Paz on July 21, 1946.

30. Getulio Vargas held power in Brazil from 1937 to 1945.

strongest party with popular support was the PIR. I was not a member of the PIR, but I was in street demonstrations, and I used to be there throwing stones.

QUESTION: The PIR was the . . . ?

SALDAÑA: Partido de la Izquierda Revolucionaria (Party of the Revolutionary Left), which later gave rise to the Communist Party. Many people who were in the PIR left to form the Communist Party.[31]

By 1952 the MNR had become the standard-bearer of the nationalization of the mines, of the agrarian reform, which had been the slogans of the PIR. The MNR came to power in 1952.

In 1950 the Communist Party was formed primarily by young people who had been members of the PIR. At that time I was living in La Paz. I participated in some actions, strikes that ended in confrontations, in massacres. That was when I began my political life, in the CP. This was in 1950. I was practically a founding member.

Becoming a miner

A student leader in the early 1950s, Saldaña was sent to Chile to attend a conference of the World Federation of Democratic Youth. Before returning he traveled to Brazil and Moscow. In the mid-1950s, as a leader of university students, he was active in fighting the efforts by the MNR government to take over the universities and abolish their autonomy.

■

Then I became a member of the Communist Party's organization commission, and in that commission we began to con-

31. There was no Communist Party in Bolivia prior to World War II. In the 1930s, supporters of the Communist International functioned in the union movement and were part of the Frente de Izquierda Boliviana (Bolivian Left Front), which in 1940 joined in forming the PIR. In 1952, following the revolutionary upsurge in Bolivia that same year, the PIR formally dissolved.

sider what to do, how to organize the party. We decided that the most important thing was to organize the party among the proletariat. But we had to consider what sectors of the proletariat were the most important, and where in the countryside we should devote special attention.

That was how we decided we had to begin in the mines. We identified the most important mines in the country at the time: Siglo XX, which had around 6,000 workers, the largest mine on the continent at that time; Potosí; and Pulacayo.

At first we did what had always been done. A leader would travel, meet with some people who belonged to the party or wanted to belong to the party, a cell would be formed, the comrade who had attended the first meeting would leave, and then nothing would happen after that. And once again we would have the same situation.

So three comrades went to these three mines to stay there about a month, find the people, meet with them, and organize the party.

But we reached the conclusion this wasn't enough. We would go, assuming we could hit all three, hold a bunch of meetings with people we had met with many times, explain the situation, and then once again the thing would evaporate. The only way to guarantee that the party would be organized for real was for us, the three of us, to enter the mines. That was how I became a miner at Siglo XX.

We also determined that we had to go inside the mines themselves, not remain outside in other sections, but to go into the very center of the mine. And so I became a miner.

The section I entered, which was made up of young men, was the specimen section. These are miners who go around in groups taking samples from the unmined locations and bringing them to the laboratory to determine what quantity of mineral the specimen contains. This was a mobile group. One day they would work here, the next day there, and the following day somewhere else. It was an ideal situation to make contact with a lot of people.

At first the specimen section had around 200 workers. Eventually the majority of the miners there became members of the party; they formed their cell and held meetings. That was where we recruited Rosendo García Maismán. So now the party existed. Then we pointed out that the party had to expand within the mine, and we said that people should transfer to different sections of the mine. But people did not want to move. In order to have the others do so, I had to set the example, and I went to the most difficult section, Block Caving.

There the amount of space was very small, and there was a lot of dust. A lot of dynamite was used, there were many explosions. In short, the work was very tough, very difficult. There are people who get silicosis after three months. Their lungs are destroyed. That's where I went.

García Maismán went to one section. And the same with other comrades, who transferred to different sections. Then the party encompassed much more. It wasn't just the specimen section, but we had party groups in other sections.

QUESTION: What years did you work there?

SALDAÑA: From 1955 until 1958.

As one might expect, I left Block Caving in very bad health. At the end of 1958 I returned to La Paz. At that time I was a member of the Central Committee.

Support to Peru, Argentina

In the early 1960s Saldaña participated in support work for guerrilla fronts trying to establish themselves in Argentina and Peru.

In late 1963 a guerrilla front was opened in Argentina, under the leadership of Jorge Ricardo Masetti, who worked under Che's direction. Masetti was an Argentine journalist who had traveled to the Sierra Maestra in Cuba in 1958 and become a supporter of the Cuban Revolution. After its victory he moved to Cuba, where he helped found the news agency Prensa Latina. Logistical support to the guerrillas in Argentina was organized from Bolivia, with the participation of Bolivian CP members. Also involved in the support work was Abelardo Colomé Ibarra (Furry), today a corps general of the Revolutionary

Armed Forces and Cuba's minister of the interior. The Argentine guer-
rillas were routed by the military in early 1964. Masetti and most of
his comrades were killed.
  Saldaña spoke about his experience.

■

After my return from the Siglo XX mine, I had an auto repair
shop, doing car repairs, paint jobs, sheet metal work, and so
on. I had the shop until the military actions began at
Ñancahuazú. Of course during this period there were times I
abandoned the shop. During that time I was giving support to
developments in the south.

QUESTION: When you say the "south". . . ?

SALDAÑA: I'm referring to Argentina. Masetti.

QUESTION: What about Peru? Were you also involved in supporting the guerrillas there?

SALDAÑA: There too.

QUESTION: Were you involved in supporting the movement
of Puerto Maldonado in Peru?

SALDAÑA: Yes. All their equipment passed through my hands.
I amassed and stored it, preparing it for shipment. My tasks
were run out of my repair shop, above all for the business of
the south. Many things were needed, and I helped resolve the
problem of packing the material for shipment. We would uti-
lize false bottoms; for example, we would take a barrel of oil,
remove the lid and fill it with items on the bottom, and cover it
up again, soldering it over and putting oil on top. When the
items reached their destination, they were opened up with a
chisel and everything was taken out.

The struggle continues

Saldaña was arrested in 1970, following the end of the revolution-
ary campaign originated by Guevara. After his release later that year,
he went to Cuba, where he stayed for twelve years, working in a fac-
tory, studying sociology and working for Radio Havana, Cuba, mak-

ing broadcasts in Quechua to Bolivia. In 1983 he returned to Bolivia, where he taught the history of political thought at the university.

■

Then came the political changes in the world, with the collapse of the socialist camp, the threats against Cuba, and the Iraq war above all. When the Iraq campaign ended they said, "Now all we need is Cuba." Remember? We thought an attack against Cuba was imminent.

So in 1990 I decided to return and occupy my modest position in the trench of defending socialism, of defending Cuba. I am here in my small trench, at a radio station where I have a regular program, and at InterPress Service, a Third World news agency.

But the attack on Cuba has not taken place, and I don't think it will. None of the enemy's predictions with respect to Cuba have been fulfilled. They have set various timetables. First it was a matter of months before Cuba fell, then within a year. Now more than ever, Cuba is rebuilding its economy. It has contacts, relations with many countries. In the United States itself there is interest in negotiating, in investing in Cuba, but the Helms-Burton Law and all the other anti-Cuban, antihuman measures do not permit it. Nevertheless Cuba moves forward, and the struggle continues.

Further reading

Castro, Fidel, "Che's Ideas Are Absolutely Relevant Today," October 1987 speech marking the twentieth anniversary of Guevara's death. Castro's speech is published together with Guevara's March 1965 article, "Socialism and Man in Cuba," in a pamphlet of that name (New York: Pathfinder, 1989). In carrying out the Bolivian campaign, Castro says, Guevara was pursuing his goal, backed by the Cuban leadership, "to return to South America . . . to make the revolution based on the experience he'd gained in our country."

Castro, Fidel, *Un encuentro con Fidel* [An encounter with Fidel] (Havana: Council of State, 1987). This book-length 1987 interview with Castro by Italian journalist Gianni Minà includes a chapter on Guevara, with an extensive section on the Bolivian campaign.

Castro, Fidel, *Selected Speeches of Fidel Castro* (New York: Pathfinder, 1979). Eight speeches by Castro from December 1961 through January 1979, including his talk on the twentieth anniversary of the Cuban Revolution.

Che Guevara, Cuba, and the Road to Socialism, in *New International* no. 8. Includes two 1963–64 articles by Che Guevara, as well as articles on Guevara's communist political legacy by Carlos Rafael Rodríguez, Carlos Tablada, Jack Barnes, Steve Clark, and Mary-Alice Waters.

Cupull, Adys and González, Froilán, *La CIA contra el Che* [The CIA versus Che] (Havana: Editora Política, 1992). Provides information on the urban underground network in Bolivia organized to support the revolutionary front led by Guevara.

Guevara, Ernesto Che, *The Bolivian Diary of Ernesto Che Guevara* (New

York: Pathfinder, 1994). A day-by-day account, written as the struggle unfolded, of the effort led by Guevara to initiate a revolutionary front in the Southern Cone of Latin America in 1966–67. Includes Fidel Castro's 1968 "A Necessary Introduction" to Guevara's diary.

Guevara, Ernesto Che, *Che Guevara Talks to Young People* (New York: Pathfinder, 2000). Eight talks by Guevara, beginning with his July 1960 speech to the opening session of the First Latin American Youth Congress in Havana. "From all the brother countries of the Americas, and from our own land," said Guevara in concluding that talk, "the voice of the peoples will answer: 'Thus it shall be: Let freedom triumph in every corner of the Americas!'" Also includes Fidel Castro's October 1997 talk in Santa Clara, Cuba, when the remains of Guevara and six other combatants in the 1966–67 guerrilla campaign—from Bolivia, Cuba, and Peru—were placed in a monument honoring their struggle.

Guevara, Ernesto Che, "Vietnam and the World Struggle for Freedom," in *Che Guevara Speaks* (New York: Pathfinder, 1967, 2000). Also known as "The Message to the Tricontinental," Guevara's last major article was written in 1966 just prior to the opening of the guerrilla campaign in Bolivia. He explains the advance of revolutionary struggles from Southeast Asia to Latin America that called for "the creation of the world's second or third Vietnam, or second *and* third Vietnam."

Guevara, Ernesto Che, *Otra vez* [Once again] (Havana: Casa Editora Abril, 2000). Guevara's account of his travels through Latin America following his graduation from medical school in 1953, culminating in his decision in Mexico to join the revolutionary movement in Cuba as troop doctor for the 1956 *Granma* expedition. Includes Guevara's reactions to the 1952 revolutionary upsurge in Bolivia after his trip to that country the following year.

Hansen, Joseph, *Dynamics of the Cuban Revolution: A Marxist Appreciation* (New York: Pathfinder, 1978). Articles written by a leader of the communist movement in the United States in defense of the Cuban Revolution as it advanced during its opening decade.

Lara, Jesús, *Guerrillero Inti* [Inti, guerrilla]. Written by a then prominent member of the Communist Party of Bolivia who was sympathetic to the 1966–68 guerrilla front led by Guevara. A firsthand account of the impact of these events within the CP.

Making History: Interviews with Four Generals of Cuba's Revolutionary Armed Forces (New York: Pathfinder, 1999). Interviews with four generals of Cuba's Revolutionary Armed Forces: Néstor López Cuba, Enrique Carreras, José Ramón Fernández, and Harry Villegas. Each with close to half a century of revolutionary activity, they recount the story of their combat experience both in Cuba and as part of internationalist missions, from Vietnam and Syria to Bolivia and Nicaragua. Edited with an introduction by Mary-Alice Waters. Preface by Juan Almeida Bosque.

Peredo, Inti, *My Campaign with Che* (published in the Pathfinder edition of *The Bolivian Diary of Ernesto Che Guevara*). An account by the central Bolivian leader of the revolutionary front led by Guevara.

Piñeiro, Manuel, *Barbarroja: Selección de testimonios y discursos del Comandante Manuel Piñeiro Losada* [Red Beard: A selection of firsthand accounts and speeches by Commander Manuel Piñeiro Losada] (Havana: Editorial Si-Mar/Tricontinental, 1999). Piñeiro was the leader in Cuba responsible for relations with the revolutionary front headed by Guevara. Using examples not previously made public, this book published after Piñeiro's death shows the extent of Cuba's support to the Bolivian effort.

The Second Declaration of Havana (New York: Pathfinder, 1962, 1994). In 1962, as the example of Cuba's socialist revolution spread throughout the Americas, the workers and farmers of Cuba responded to Washington's newly imposed economic embargo by issuing an uncompromising call for a continent-wide revolutionary struggle.

Secretos de generales [Secrets of generals] (Havana: Fuerzas Armadas Revolucionarias, 1997). Interviews with forty-one generals of the Revolutionary Armed Forces. They recount experiences during Cuba's revolutionary war, the 1961 battle at Playa Girón, internationalist missions, and other efforts to defend and strengthen the Cuban Revolution. Includes interview with Abelardo Colomé Ibarra (*Furry*) on his participation in the 1963–64 guerrilla front in Argentina with which Saldaña collaborated from Bolivia. Edited by Luis Báez.

Villegas, Harry, *Pombo: A Man of Che's 'guerrilla'* (New York: Pathfinder,

1997). The diary and account of the 1966–68 revolutionary struggle in Bolivia, written by Harry Villegas. Villegas, whose nom de guerre is *Pombo*, served on the general staff throughout the eleven-month Bolivian campaign and was one of three surviving Cuban combatants.

Villegas, Harry, *At the Side of Che Guevara* (New York: Pathfinder, 1997). Two interviews with Villegas on the strategic course and political lessons of the revolutionary front in Bolivia led by Guevara.

Waters, Mary-Alice, *Che Guevara and the Imperialist Reality* (New York: Pathfinder, 1998). Based on a presentation to a 1997 Havana conference marking the thirtieth anniversary of the revolutionary campaign in Bolivia. The event was sponsored by *Tricontinental* magazine, in which the talks by Waters and other conference participants appeared.

Most of the titles above are available from Pathfinder, 410 West Street, New York, NY 10014.

Index

CUBA and the Latin American revolution

The Bolivian Diary of Ernesto Che Guevara

Guevara's day-by-day chronicle of the 1966–67 guerrilla campaign in Bolivia, an effort to forge a continent-wide revolutionary movement of workers and peasants and open the road to socialist revolution in South America.
Includes—for the first time in English—*My Campaign with Che* by Bolivian leader Inti Peredo. Introduction by Mary-Alice Waters. $21.95

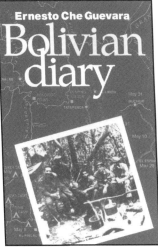

Making History

Interviews with Four Generals of Cuba's Revolutionary Armed Forces

Through the stories of four outstanding Cuban generals, each with close to half a century of revolutionary activity, we can see the class dynamics that have shaped our entire epoch. We can understand how the people of Cuba, as they struggle to build a new society, have for more than forty years held Washington at bay. Preface by Juan Almeida; introduction by Mary-Alice Waters. $15.95. Also in Spanish.

To Speak the Truth

Why Washington's 'Cold War' against Cuba Doesn't End

FIDEL CASTRO AND CHE GUEVARA

In historic speeches before the United Nations and UN bodies, Guevara and Castro address the workers of the world, explaining why the U.S. government so hates the example set by the socialist revolution in Cuba and why Washington's effort to destroy it will fail. $16.95

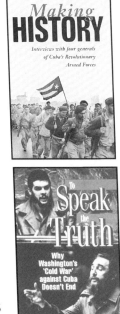

WRITE FOR A FREE CATALOG

The Second Declaration of Havana

With the First Declaration of Havana

Two manifestos of the Cuban people to the oppressed and exploited throughout the Americas. The first declaration was proclaimed in September 1960. The second declaration, in February 1962, calls for continent-wide revolutionary struggle. "What does the Cuban revolution teach?" it asks. "That revolution is possible." $4.50.
Also available in Spanish and French.

CHE GUEVARA TALKS TO YOUNG PEOPLE

Che Guevara Talks to Young People

In eight talks between 1959 and 1964, the Argentine-born revolutionary challenges youth of Cuba and the world to read and to study, to work and become disciplined. To join the front lines of struggles, small and large. To politicize their organizations and in the process politicize themselves. To become a different kind of human being as they strive together with working people of all lands to transform the world. And, along this line of march, to revel in the spontaneity and joy of being young. $14.95. In Spanish and English.

Che Guevara AND THE Imperialist Reality
Mary-Alice Waters

Che Guevara and the Imperialist Reality

MARY-ALICE WATERS

"The world of capitalist disorder—the imperialist reality of the 21st century—would not be strange to Che," Waters explains. "Far from being dismayed by the odds we face, he would have examined the world with scientific precision and charted a course to win." $3.00. In English and Spanish.

Che Guevara, Cuba, and the Road to Socialism

ARTICLES BY ERNESTO CHE GUEVARA, CARLOS RAFAEL RODRÍGUEZ, CARLOS TABLADA, MARY-ALICE WATERS, STEVE CLARK, JACK BARNES
Exchanges from the early 1960s and today on the political perspectives defended by Guevara as he helped lead working people to advance the transformation of economic and social relations in Cuba.
In *New International* no. 8. $10.00

Pombo: A Man of Che's *guerrilla*
With Che Guevara in Bolivia, 1966–68

A never-before published story of the 1966–68 revolutionary campaign in Bolivia led by Ernesto Che Guevara. This is the diary and account of Pombo—a young fighter, still in his 20s, who was a member of Guevara's general staff. Harry Villegas is today a brigadier general in Cuba's Revolutionary Armed Forces. Villegas's account of this epic chapter in the history of the Americas foreshadows the titanic class battles that will mark the 21st century. $21.95

Dynamics of the Cuban Revolution
A Marxist Appreciation

JOSEPH HANSEN
How did the Cuban revolution come about? Why does it represent, as Hansen puts it, an "unbearable challenge" to U.S. imperialism? What political challenges has it confronted? Written as the revolution advanced from its earliest days. $20.95

New International

A MAGAZINE OF MARXIST POLITICS AND THEORY

U.S. Imperialism Has Lost the Cold War

...That's what the Socialist Workers Party concluded at the opening of the 1990s, in the wake of the collapse of regimes and parties across Eastern Europe and in the USSR that claimed to be communist. Contrary to imperialism's hopes, the working class in those countries had not been crushed. It remains an intractable obstacle to reimposing and stabilizing capitalist relations, one that will have to be confronted by the exploiters in class battles—in a hot war.

Issue no. 11 of *New International* analyzes the propertied rulers' failed expectations and explains why the historic odds in favor of the working class have increased, not diminished, at the opening of the 21st century. $14.00

Imperialism's March toward Fascism and War

Jack Barnes

"There will be new Hitlers, new Mussolinis. That is inevitable. What is not inevitable is that they will triumph. The working-class vanguard will organize our class to fight back against the devastating toll we are made to pay for the capitalist crisis. The future of humanity will be decided in the contest between these contending class forces."—Jack Barnes, "Imperialism's March toward Fascism and War." In *New International* no. 10. $14.00

Opening Guns of World War III
Washington's Assault on Iraq
Jack Barnes

The U.S. government's murderous assault on Iraq heralded increasingly sharp conflicts among imperialist powers, the rise of rightist and fascist forces, growing instability of international capitalism, and more wars. In *New International* no. 7. Also includes "1945: When U.S. Troops Said, No!" by Mary-Alice Waters. $12.00

The Second Assassination of Maurice Bishop
Steve Clark

The lead article in *New International* no. 6 reviews the accomplishments of the 1979–83 revolution in the Caribbean island of Grenada. Explains the roots of the 1983 coup that led to the murder of revolutionary leader Maurice Bishop, and to the destruction of the workers and farmers government by a Stalinist political faction within the governing New Jewel Movement.

Also in *New International* no. 6: Washington's Domestic Contra Operation by *Larry Seigle*. $15.00

The Rise and Fall of the Nicaraguan Revolution

Lessons for revolutionists from the workers and farmers government that came to power in Nicaragua in July 1979. Based on ten years of socialist journalism from inside Nicaragua, this special issue of *New International* number 9 recounts the achievements and worldwide impact of the Nicaraguan revolution. It then traces the political retreat of the Sandinista National Liberation Front leadership that led to the downfall of the revolution in the closing years of the 1980s. Documents of the Socialist Workers Party by *Jack Barnes, Steve Clark*, and *Larry Seigle*. $14.00

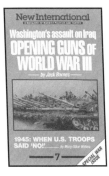

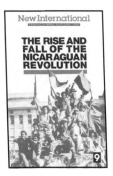

Also from Pathfinder

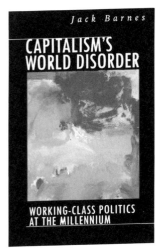

Capitalism's World Disorder

Working-Class Politics at the Millennium

JACK BARNES

The social devastation, financial panic, political turmoil, police brutality, and acts of imperialist aggression accelerating around us are not chaos. They are the product of lawful—and understandable— forces unleashed by capitalism. But the future the propertied classes have in store for us is not inevitable. It can be changed by the timely solidarity, courageous action, and united struggle of workers and farmers conscious of their power to transform the world. $23.95. Also available in Spanish and French.

The Changing Face of U.S. Politics

Working-Class Politics and the Trade Unions

JACK BARNES

A handbook for the new generations coming into the factories, mines, and mills, as they react to the uncertain life, ceaseless turmoil, and brutality of capitalism. It shows how millions of working people, as political resistance grows, will revolutionize themselves, their unions and other organizations, and their conditions of life and work. Also available in Spanish and French. $19.95

The Communist Manifesto

KARL MARX AND FREDERICK ENGELS

Founding document of the modern working-class movement, published in 1848. Explains why communism is derived not from preconceived principles but from facts, from proletarian movements springing from the actual class struggle. $3.95. Also available in Spanish.

Write for a catalog. See front of book for addresses.

Malcolm X Talks to Young People

"I for one will join in with anyone, I don't care what color you are, as long as you want to change this miserable condition that exists on this earth"—Malcolm X, December 1964.
Also includes his 1965 interview with the *Young Socialist* magazine. $10.95

Socialism on Trial

JAMES P. CANNON

The basic ideas of socialism, explained in testimony during the trial of 18 leaders of the Minneapolis Teamsters union and the Socialist Workers Party framed up and imprisoned under the notorious Smith "Gag" Act during World War II. $15.95. Also available in Spanish.

Puerto Rico: Independence Is a Necessity

RAFAEL CANCEL MIRANDA

In two interviews, Puerto Rican independence leader Cancel Miranda—one of five Puerto Rican Nationalists imprisoned by Washington for more than 25 years until 1979—speaks out on the brutal reality of U.S. colonial domination, the campaign to free Puerto Rican political prisoners, the example of Cuba's socialist revolution, and the resurgence of the independence movement today. $3.00. Also available in Spanish.

The Revolution Betrayed

What Is the Soviet Union and Where Is It Going?

LEON TROTSKY

In 1917 the working class and peasantry of Russia were the motor force for one of the most profound revolutions in history. Yet within ten years a political counterrevolution by a privileged social layer whose chief spokesperson was Joseph Stalin was being consolidated. This classic study of the Soviet workers state and its degeneration illuminates the roots of the social and political crisis shaking the former Soviet Union today. $19.95. Also available in Spanish and Russian.

Teamster Rebellion

FARRELL DOBBS

The 1934 strikes that built the industrial union movement in Minneapolis and helped pave the way for the CIO, recounted by a central leader of that battle. The first in a four-volume series on the class-struggle leadership of the strikes and organizing drives that transformed the Teamsters union in much of the Midwest into a fighting social movement and pointed the road toward independent labor political action. $16.95

Socialism: Utopian and Scientific

FREDERICK ENGELS

Modern socialism is not a doctrine, Engels explains, but a working-class movement growing out of the establishment of large-scale capitalist industry and its social consequences. $4.00

To See the Dawn

Baku, 1920—First Congress
of the Peoples of the East
How can peasants and workers in the colonial world achieve freedom from imperialist exploitation? By what means can working people overcome divisions incited by their national ruling classes and act together for their common class interests? These questions were addressed by 2,000 delegates to the 1920 Congress of the Peoples of the East. $19.95

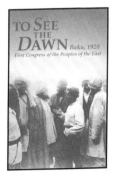

The Jewish Question

A Marxist Interpretation
ABRAM LEON

Traces the historical rationalizations of anti-Semitism to the fact that Jews—in the centuries preceding the domination of industrial capitalism—were forced to become a "people-class" of merchants and moneylenders. Leon explains why the propertied rulers incite renewed Jew-hatred today. $17.95

Lenin's Final Fight

Speeches and Writings, 1922–23

V.I. LENIN

In the early 1920s Lenin waged a political battle in the leadership of the Communist Party of the USSR to maintain the course that had enabled the workers and peasants to overthrow the tsarist empire, carry out the first successful socialist revolution, and begin building a world communist movement. The issues posed in Lenin's political fight remain at the heart of world politics today. $19.95. Also available in Spanish.

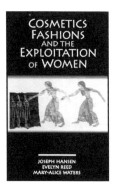

Cosmetics, Fashions, and the Exploitation of Women

JOSEPH HANSEN, EVELYN REED, AND MARY-ALICE WATERS

How big business promotes cosmetics to generate profits and perpetuate the oppression of women. The introduction by Waters explains how the entry of millions of women into the workforce during and after World War II irreversibly changed U.S. society and laid the basis for a renewed rise of struggles for women's equality. $14.95

Thomas Sankara Speaks

The Burkina Faso Revolution, 1983–87

Peasants and workers in the West African country of Burkina Faso established a popular revolutionary government and began to combat the hunger, illiteracy, and economic backwardness imposed by imperialist domination. Thomas Sankara, who led that struggle, explains the example set for all of Africa. $19.95

From Pathfinder